The Force Revealed:
Real Life Applications of the Force and the Art of the Jedi Mind Trick

By Doug Valiant

Table of Contents

◆ Forward

◆ Chapter 1: Behold The Force

  ○ Section 1: Understanding the Force
  ○ Section 2: The Force through the Ages
  ○ Section 3: The Force and You
  ○ Section 4: Manifestations of the Force

◆ Chapter 2: Force Persuasion and the Art of the Jedi Mind Trick

  ○ Section 1: Force Influence
  ○ Section 2: The Force and the Mind
  ○ Section 3: Method to the Mind Trick
  ○ Section 4: Purpose in the Trick
  ○ Section 5: Force Listening: The Art of Hearing Thoughts.

◆ Chapter 3: Behind the Shadow of the Force: Force Intuition and the Psychology of the Force

  ○ Section 1: The Psychology Behind Force Powers
  ○ Section 2: Force Intuition: Creating the Illusion of Clairvoyance
  ○ Section 3: The Feint: Making Use of Subjective Validation
  ○ Section 4: The Great Escape
  ○ Section 5: Bounded by Words

◆ Chapter 4: Numinations: The Language of the Force

   ○ Section 1: Numination: The Act of Subconscious Communication
   ○ Section 2: Monkey See Monkey Do
   ○ Section 3: The Numonic Lexicon: The Vocabulary of the Force
   ○ Section 4: Numonic Grammer: The Syntax of the Force
      ▪ Introductory Force Flow
      ▪ Conjection
      ▪ Elusive Intention
      ▪ Missing Reference
      ▪ Vital Techniques
   ○ Section 5: Numinetics: The use of Body Language with Subconsious Communication.
      ▪ The Numinetic Probe
      ▪ Head Gesticulation
      ▪ Visage
      ▪ Eye Cues
      ▪ The Breath
      ▪ Numinetic Projection

◆ Chapter 5: Secret of the Seers: Putting it All Together

   ○ Section 1: A Sequence of Actions
   ○ Section 2: It's All in How You Ask
   ○ Section 3: If They Don't Confirm Your Statement
   ○ Section 4: The Force Binds Us
   ○ Section 5: Equations to Secret of the Seer

◆ Chapter 6: Final Understandings of the Force and its Power

   ○ Section 1: The Use of Non-Force Equals Access to the Force
   ○ Section 2: Conditioning and the Force
   ○ Section 3: The Duality of the Force

Foreword

Hello and welcome to your future. I imagine, right now, as you see these words that you are wondering to yourself just what exactly is inside this book. What kind of secrets does it hold? You may also be wondering how some of these powers can be real. Let me assure you. There is a lock on the door to these mysteries and in your hand right now you are holding the key.

Have you ever wondered why you were intrigued by the power known as the Force? Why you had an attraction to it. It is the same reason you picking up this book was no mere accident. We both know that you picked this book up because you are curious and you want to know more, but there is another reason, one that you might have overlooked. You picked it up because you have the gift inside you, the gift of the Force.

You may be skeptical but haven't you always had a feeling that there was something different about you? A feeling deep inside that you have had all your life. A feeling that you're supposed to do something. You don't know what it is but it is there. You might have even learned to try and ignore it for some reason, but have you ever asked yourself why? Why you have felt this way?

I know you like to imagine possibilities, don't you? I bet when you were younger you did it even more. Have you ever wondered why you didn't follow through on some of them? It is because we have been trained not to. We have been trained to accept what advertisers, the media and society accepts as the norm. This socialization has kept you from your true potential and has quieted the power of the Force inside you. But it is still there and it flows inside your veins. Together with some help from this book we will break down the walls of those social limitations and bring you your inherent power, the awesome power that is The Force.

Chapter 1:

Behold The Force

A long long time ago in the mind of an ingenious and brilliant man came an epic story....
STAR WARS!!! .

With this story came a belief, a belief in an unforeseeable power that connects all things. The
idea of an energy field that is formed by the fabric life itself, an enigma far beyond technological
understanding, a power that is so limitless in its magnitude it could be considered the very thread of the
universe itself. This profound belief was the belief in The Force!

> *"For my ally is The Force. And a powerful ally it is. Life creates it, makes it*
> *grow. The Force surrounds us and binds us. Luminous beings are we, not this*
> *crude matter. You must feel The Force around you. Here, between you, me, the*
> *tree, the rock...everywhere, even between the land and the ship."*
>
> *Yoda*

Can you imagine what it would be like to be able to channel this remarkable power through you? To have a power so remarkable that it would appear to others that you had the amazing ability of clairvoyance or even telepathy. A power that enabled you to do the things in your imagination that you never before thought were possible.

Believe it or not it is possible for you to obtain this mysterious gift that binds the universe together and flows inside all of life. You can connect with it and have it connect with you. You can have this amazing gift because it exists. It may not exist in an actual physical sense however it does exist. It exists inside you, me, your teacher when you were a child, the tree outside that is bustling in the breeze, and in all the living things around you. You know this to be true, deep down inside to the very core of your soul, you know. You have always known. You have always known that there was something unique about you but you just couldn't put your finger on it. It is the fact that deep down you know that there is an unknown force that exists inside all life because if you didn't you wouldn't be reading this right now.

Have you ever asked yourself what really attracted you to the stories or wondered why you found Yoda's words to be so wise? It is because of The Force. The Force has brought you up to this point and now it is time for you to learn more. Now is the time to put away the illusion's and conditioned view's of the false reality you had been shown because those false impressions of reality will only lead you to a path of disappointment and suffering.

"You must unlearn what you have learned."

Yoda

The true Force behind the universe can be yours, it is possible, it exists, and it can be yours to wield. However, to channel it requires total dedication and a separation from the world of your past. Now is the time to receive the message you were always meant to hear, because it is your destiny. It is your time, your time to begin learning about the astonishing power known as The Force.

Section 1:

Understanding The Force

Understanding the power of Force and wielding it are two very different things. To be able to use The Force first must come the understanding of it and then one can wield its awesome power. The power of The Force can elicit some amazing abilities from some people. Many of these powers seem like magic but with recent advances in science one will find that they are not all that mysterious or magical at all. These powers are just your latent abilities that you have just not yet tapped into, and with the help of my teachings you will be able to open that power that has been dormant inside of you for so many years.

With the power of The Force you will be able to do many astounding feats. The Force touches everything and manifests itself insides ones thoughts and feelings. Knowing this basic principal of The Force, it is easy to realize that knowledge of The Force will allow you access inside other people's minds to see their hidden thoughts and feelings as well. Because of this The Force can also provide you with the profound ability to command the will of others and magically direct their reasoning. The Force is the wisest of advisors and will guide you when the way before you is unclear.

9

"Let your actions be guided by The Force and it will bring light upon the

things to come."

Doug Valiant

By accepting its guidance it allows you to seek a noble vision of one's inner nature and of one's ultimate potential. Allowing the power of The Force to guide your life will also reveal the path to end the struggle in life and reveal how to flow with life instead. It will navigate you through the path of confusion, because following The Force's guidance sets ones mind free from clutter enabling one to experience what their life truly is and allowing one to see their true destiny.

The Force will even award you with the ability to foresee the future actions of others as well.

The Force is the pure energy of awareness and though The Force flows through every living thing, it can only be harnessed by rigorous training of your mind to create that awareness. The mind holds within it vital information much more than you are ever truly aware of. Training this awareness is essential to your growth with The Force because when you become aware of The Force you have the ability to become conscious of all things, places and even time. Therefore it must be said that awareness, experience and training will be the most vital elements of concentration if you intend to harness the power of that which is The Force.

The Force is most powerful when it is connected with the ideals of compassion and valor. The best way to manifest it is to live in harmony with the world around you, yet not succeed to its

10

conventions. Flow with it and avoid the folly of status quo and the failings of vanity. Work with what The Force guides you to do and not just your mind. It is better to make no distinctions of how you think things should be as compared to how they actually are because emotional fervor can override your rationality and misguide you. Let go of conceit. Remember to live in harmony with everything around you, because The Force touches every living thing and doesn't just flow from all of us, but through all of us as well. These principal insights will help in you understand things more when using The Force and will help you create a stronger connection with it as well.

Section 2:

The Force through the Ages

Some people may be wondering how this idea from a fictional movie can be true. Well it is real and it has been around much longer than the movie in terms of the belief. It always was and will be, is the true essence of The Force. It has gone by various different names throughout time; Mana, Baraka, Chi, Numen, Asha, Teotl and Grace to name a few. Some of the core fundamentals of The Force have also been found in many long time belief systems such as Buddhism, plus the Tao, even within the Bible, Koran and Torah there is mention of it.

It is believed that The Force resides in all life. In the Tao they call it Chi. Chi is an energy that flows through life and the Tao is the way to tap that energy. Balance between the duality of the light

and dark side of The Force can be associated to the Tao's symbol of Yin and Yang. The Yin and Yang symbolize the true nature of things and the Tao encompasses the universe and all living things just as The Force does.

In certain forms of Paganism they believe that the incarnation of life force manifests itself in nature, and they can channel those life forces through themselves and in turn affect their surroundings.

In Islam Baraka is an energy guided by the hand of the divine that flows between all living things even through the boundaries of time itself. It is the energy that gives one luck or blessings to one's actions. Just like the Grace of God in Christianity. In Christianity the unseen deity of the Father will lead those who have faith in him.

The Ancient Aztecs also believed in an active unforeseen energy of divinity that they referred to as Teotl. They believed that all things are Teotl and that everything and everything is connected to it. Teotl is what unifies all things from life and death to light and dark, much like the Tao. This unity is the essence of the entire universe.

In Zen Buddhism there is a belief that all things have Buddha nature, meaning that all things have the ability to become enlightened. The sole purpose in Zen is to let go of ones ego to reach a higher state of awareness. There is no past or future there is only now. Zen is a way that concentrates on direct experience rather than on dogma or scripture. Many Zen practitioners believe that wisdom is not passed through words in and of them selves, but through the transmission of Zen enlightenment by having mindfulness.

Section 3:

The Force and You.

As all these beliefs have established the power of The Force does exists and has done so throughout recorded time. The Force can flow into you and with my help you will be able to work with this amazing power in the world around you. I will teach you how to manifest this by training you in the ways of The Force and giving you information on how to recondition your mind to become aware of numerous things that people ignore.

In this book are many secrets, techniques and scientific studies that explain why The Force works. As stated before Force Powers are not some supernatural ability that a comic book superhero may have. Force Powers are natural powers that we have been taught to ignore but they still reside in us and can be cultivated. In this book I will show you that the Powers of The Force are naturally inherent and can be manifested through specialized conditioning of the psyche and having strong mental control.

"Hmm, control, control. You must learn control."

Yoda

Greatness comes through the means of The Force and within this book lays many of the developmental techniques for learning how to use the Force. You goal is to manifest a connection with The Force; you will do this by thorough review of the techniques mentioned inside these pages as well as paying close attention to your results. It will take a great deal of discipline and much practice for you to become proficient with The Force.

Just like a martial art it is important that you repeat these techniques often and with diligence so you will become a master at them. Your goal is to make their use a habit in your everyday life. This will strengthen your relationship, or oneness, with The Force and will allow you to channel its power as if it was an extension of yourself. Just like your arms or your legs are a part of you The Force is also a part of you. You just are not that connected to it because you have never been taught how to realize how to be connected to it.

Let me ask you a question if your leg was cut off does that make that leg not yours just because you are not connected to it still? The answer is of course is, that it is still your leg. It is the connection to it that allowed you to control it. Like your leg when you are connected to The Force you also can control it as well.

Think about a child learning to walk it is not use to using its legs and therefore maybe a little bit clumsy at first however after some time the child will walk and maybe even later learn to dance. It is the same as with The Force. Your connection with it will increase exponentially by a commitment to the training and with deep reflection upon your results. With a deeper connection comes a stronger control. This in and of itself will enhance your ability to achieve a state of mental, emotional, and physical harmony, with the great Force and giving you the ability to dance.

At first you may find some of the practices or concepts in this book not so easy to understand or even accomplish for that matter. You may even initially meet with failure and this could cause a bit of

14

frustration. This is a perfectly normal reaction for one who is just beginning to learn these techniques. It will take discipline, fortitude and strength to get beyond that hurtle and to the point where these skills become second nature to you, but realize deep down inside that they will come.

"No! Try not. Do, or do not. There is no try."

Yoda

Limits on The Force are made only by your amount of dedication you put into its practice. Understand that awareness, experience and training are vital and extremely important assets if you want to harness the power of The Force, for the way of The Force is beyond our traditional education and normal understanding yet it should not be feared. One must be prepared to put fear, regret, and uncertainty aside. Vital energy is sapped by such emotions. By shedding their weight the power of The Force can flow through you and reveal to you your unlimited potential.

Section 4:

Manifestations of The Force

It is known that Force Powers can bring to light inherent mental abilities and enhance physical prowess. If you have seen the movies, read the books, or even played the video games you will know that there are many kinds of Force Powers, but several of the sources from which those powers originate have not yet been discovered. Since we do not have all the knowledge as of how to accomplish every one of The Force Powers in the movies and books, in this book we are going to focus on some of the powers we do have knowledge of and that is extra sensory Force Powers. These are Force Powers like the Jedi Mind Trick, Force Intuition and Force Persuasion.

These Force Sensory Powers I am talking about refer to the field of the Force that influences the thoughts and minds of others as well as enhance ones own awareness, providing one with inexplicable insights. These powers are used to induce specific thoughts into others by specific Force inspired wording and subtle non verbal communication. Manifestations of these Force powers will often be viewed as forms of clairvoyance and telepathy by others. However they are merely untapped mental abilities of perception and neural conditioning. If one becomes proficient at it one will be able to transfer thought without the use of speech after a while and communicate only through subconscious micro movements of the face and body. Much like how sometimes when you and someone you are fairly familiar with know what the other is thinking with just a glace. Our goal is to condition these types of responses so they become a natural part of your everyday life.

Take note that when you are doing the techniques in the book you are also training your intuition, which is the main goal, this is essential to mastering The Force.

> *"Do not come to rely on The Force to the detriment of your other senses*
>
> *and abilities."*
>
> *Obi Wan Kenobi*

It is said that The Force is the fabric of life and only through complete acceptance of The Force can one achieve total freedom. With a deep understanding of this one will be able to harness and work with its amazing power in the world around them. That is best done by avoiding confrontation, by

16

attempting to resolve matters in a more peaceful manner by using The Force, instead of having senseless arguments or conflicts that will slowly drain ones life force away.

Dedication to your ultimate potential is made by accepting the fact that the most gallant act that one can ever accomplish is the acceptance of The Force. Remember you are in the hands of something far greater than you could ever imagine, so enjoy learning the secrets of this wonderful gift and use them wisely.

Chapter 2:

Force Persuasion and the Art of the Jedi Mind Trick:

In the epic story of Star Wars there was an interesting way certain Jedi had of using The Force to influence others. This interesting use of The Force was called the Jedi Mind Trick.

In the movie Star Wars: A New Hope, Obi Wan Kenobi used this Jedi Mind Trick on one the guards at Mos Eisley with some remarkable results. What happened was that Imperial Stormtroopers were looking for some missing droids with plans to the Deathstar in them and stopped Obi Wan and his entourage, which included thus said droids. At this time Obi Wan proceeded to use the Jedi Mind Trick and avoided having the droids being confiscated. This was such a popular scene that we are now left with his infamous quote "These aren't the droids you're looking for."

When using a Jedi Mind Trick, a Jedi would often times say something using a certain tone of voice and accompany it with a slight gesture such as a wave their hand. Subsequently the listener would automatically concede to whatever was being told to them without having the ability to think for them selves and immediately do whatever the Jedi had suggested. Many times, the listener would enter a state of confusion about why they had their new formed opinion, nonetheless they would maintain thus said opinion anyway. You can personally observe this happening in the movie Star Wars: Return of the Jedi when Luke Skywalker persuaded Bib Fortuna to take him to Jaba the Hutt on the planet Dagobah.

When learning the Jedi Mind Trick you should realize that the Jedi Mind trick is just a technique associated to a discipline in The Force called Force Persuasion. Force Persuasion is a field of Force Sensory powers that are used to influence the thoughts and minds of other beings. Often times Mind Tricks were used to sway someone into some sort of agreement by a simple suggestion while using voice and word manipulation. Mind Tricks can also be used to cause another person to divulge

some kind of information that they may not typically want to reveal. This ability is useful in a many respects and provides its practitioners a method of resolving matters in a peaceful non-violent way. Because The Force is connected to all living things this is the best way of strengthening the Power of The Force within you.

The Jedi Mind Trick is just one of the many skills that you can perform using Force Persuasion. Force Persuasion can be also used to preprogram some of the actions of another however this is an advance application of the technique and my take years to acquire. The reason the Jedi Mind Trick is popular is because of how easy it is to learn. As you learn more about what Force Persuasion is and how to use it you will find ways to create your own "Tricks" and apply them to your own arsenal.

As stated before the Jedi Mind Trick is just one form of Force Persuasion and Force Persuasion is a very powerful skill that is not very instinctual, so it must be learned and learning it will not be a simple task for just anyone, but if one has capability and desire to learn its secrets then one will be able to master these powers.

To understand one's mind is the first step toward making The Force a part of one's life. If one is not willing to invest one's energy in mastering The Force, and instead squanders it in chasing external rewards, one will lose power over one's life, and end up becoming a reactionary instrument of circumstance.

There will be academic skills that need to be applied while learning to understand and master Force Sensory skills such as; Social-Psychology, Neurology, Mentalism, and the study of Hypnosis. This is because one must use their mind to apply these skills so one must need to know how the mind works as well, hence the word mind in the name Jedi "Mind" Trick.

One will need to Focus on their end results and accept that with great strides one reaps great rewards. In the end one will be granted the power that is The Force.

Section 1:

Force Influence

What is Force Influence? Force Influence is an indirect, and on occasion direct, communication technique that allows you to bypass conscious awareness and communicate directly to a person's subconscious mind by use of The Force and it is the main component behind the Jedi Mind Trick. The Force is our power and our ally and the subconscious mind is a direct link to this power. Its awareness holds all the information of one's life within it and with that the life's energy. Our thoughts and actions channeled through the power of The Force are able to shape destiny. As stated before The Force doesn't just flow from all of us, but through all of us as well, so the awareness is a stream and one should learn to make use of it.

Typically most people are unaware of this power that lies behind the actions of their subconscious mind so they only pay attention to their thought processes running in their conscious minds. Let me show you an example how this works; you are obviously aware that you consciously make a choice when you decide to go on a trip. You also consciously choose to speak when you feel like you want to. You consciously choose to eat the foods you want to eat, and you consciously chose to wear the clothes you want to wear. However you are not consciously choosing when to blink now are you? You are not consciously deciding the beat of your heart either. These are the acts of your subconscious mind, it has an overlooked connection to The Force and it actually has the ability to do far more than just those simple yet very important tasks.

The subconscious mind is what does much of the hidden grunt work for you. It is like your personal helper with a direct connection to The Force. If you ask yourself "Why am I so great?" You subconscious mind will go into the limitless awareness of your life's history and find all the reasons why, just because you asked it to. When you become aware of the subconscious's connection with The Force, you have the potential to perceive all things; all places, all people and even all time associated with that connecting life force.

Your subconscious is connected to The Force and because The Force has a vast stock of information your subconscious mind is also an amazing problem solver, it is what helps you make coherent sentences, remember how to ride a bike, and it preplans ideas before you even think about them. That is how sometimes you can just come up with an idea that works on the first try or why you just knew how to get somewhere even though you have never been there before. Like an unforeseen guardian The Force can guide you through your journey during life. These abilities come to play because your subconscious mind is linked directly to The Force and has already analyzed and planed the situation for you.

The subconscious mind has many other important attributes; it automates many of your regular everyday activities like regulating your heartbeat and your breathing patterns. It even helps you drive your car. Do you remember when you first learned to drive a car and how you were a bit shaky with the wheel? That was because you were more consciously controlling the wheel at the time because it was new. However after a while you didn't have to think about how you held the wheel it just came natural to you. That is because your subconscious conditioned the physical information you gave it and made it automatic.

In other words your subconscious is the hidden power behind the person, it does most of the leg work so you can concentrate on other more important things, like this book. Your conscious mind needs to be able to concentrate because it gives you the ability to; control action, focus attention and evaluate ideas, then it processes and transmits this information back into the subconscious mind so it can deal with it afterwards.

Now, what if there was a power that enabled you to circumvent the evaluating and decision making conscious mind and communicate directly into the subconscious mind without the person even being aware of it? Do you think that would be a valuable skill to have? Do you think you would want to use it? Well, that is exactly what Force Influence does. By the use of Force Powers Force Influence bisects conscious evaluations and goes right to the subconscious mind and allows you to implant some decisions or evaluations for yourself.

Force Influence is actual a form of social influence techniques combined with hypnosis to directly communicate to the subconscious mind. The hypnosis that is used is not like the hypnosis you see in the movies or television with the silly looking guy who puts people into zombie like states with a pocket watch swinging in his hand saying "You are getting sleepy." Force Influence is based on a form of hypnosis that allows you to work directly with the subconscious and its decision making abilities while the subject is completely awake and conscious. This is because there are two distinctively different types of hypnosis that exist; there is one which is called Light Hypnosis and another named Deep Hypnosis. Under the type of hypnosis called Light Hypnosis the listener is awake but goes into a state of trace while you are speaking to them. As opposed to Deep Hypnosis which is the type hypnosis where you see someone put into a sleep like state and avoid dealing with conscious interference. Using Force Influence we want the listener to be awake so we can interact with them this is why Force

23

Influence is based on Light Hypnosis and not deep hypnosis.

Force Influence is founded on a neuropsychological phenomenon sometimes called disassociated control. Disassociated Control starts in the anterior 24ingulated cortex region of the brain. The Anterior Cingulate Cortex (ACC) is the back part of Cingulate Cortex which is located behind the Prefrontal Cortex and is in charge of rational functions such as error recognition, problem solving, emotional self control, as well as many autonomic functions like regulating blood pressure and heart rate. The ACC plays a crucial role in intelligent behavior and decision making. How this happens is that the Anterior Cingulate Cortex becomes active when people translate words into meanings. During this translation the brain divides its processing power between both the words being said and the meanings that are derived from them. This action is generated by two separate independent paths of perception one being cognitive processing (Conscious mind) and the other autonomic functioning (Subconscious mind). This process explains why one path of perception can be aware of something, while simultaneously the other path of perception is completely unaware of that exact same something. This is because one of the paths of perceptions has had its focus diverted on to something other than the original something. Why is this important? Well because the subconscious is the regulatory activator of people's autonomic functions. With that being said to have the ability to communicate directly to somebody's subconscious mind, without conscious interpretation, will directly influence the decisions being made by that person ala the Jedi Mind Trick.

This is done by channeling The Force and using subconscious communication skills (Numinations) that have seemingly normal conversational grammar so you can access the listener's subconscious mind. The way it works is that you will have a normal conversation yet employ techniques that conjure The Force and cause a shift in the listeners brain wave function while you are

24

speaking with them. Using these carefully crafted techniques in grammar and inflection (Numinations) you will be able to avert conscious attention to the immediate conversation while at the same time slipping in subconscious suggestions to the listener. The major keys to accomplishing this are by being ambiguous, conditioning the listener and by employing culturally assumed meanings (socialization). All three are keys that set the persons mind up to make conscious assertions out of habit while ignoring other potential meanings. To garner the power of The Force and become a master of Force Influence you will have to develop the skills of Numination (the art of subconscious communication) and that will be discussed in greater detail later on in the book.

Section 2:

The Force and the Mind

For right now I would like to backtrack a little bit and educate you some more about the importance of brainwaves and their effects on people's minds. This part is somewhat technical but it is important to know when employing The Force because knowing the mind allows you control of the mind.

In order for the brain to work it produces what we call brainwaves. These are electrical signals that work in frequencies and are rated by cycles per second it is similar to how your heart pumps blood in a way. As the Heart beats blood at so many beats per minute so does the brain send electrical signals at cycles per second and those cycles create certain frequencies. These frequencies often times vary and have a direct affect the current state of ones mind. That means that how conscious or unconscious someone is dependant on the speed of the brainwave frequencies at that precise moment. These frequencies are represented by something called hertz levels and many different states of mind are also measured by these hertz levels.

Using EEGs (Electroencephalogram- a test that measures and records the electrical activity of the brain) researchers have found that the specific brainwaves can be attributed to certain states of mind. For instance when you are alert and making decisions you are in what we call Beta which is signified by a frequency of 12-30Hz. When you are asleep you are usually in Delta which is 3Hz and below. Theta is 4-7Hz and the frequency typically associated with deep relaxation, falling asleep and what most people are more familiar with when we talk about hypnosis. The last set of frequencies is Alpha 8-12Hz and this will be the one we will be focusing on when it comes to Force Persuasion.

Beta (12-30Hz)   Fully Awake

          Conscious Decisions

          Alert

Alpha (8-12Hz)   Relaxed

          Daydreaming

          Zoning Out.

Theta (4-7Hz)   Falling Asleep

          Deep Relaxation

Delta (0.5-4Hz)   Deep Sleep

          Unconscious

26

Alpha is a state that is also associated with light hypnosis but not the deep hypnosis that you see on television shows. No, this is the hypnosis that mentalists, certain religious organizations, and the media use to create a direct pathway to your subconscious mind. The Alpha state is the neurological state that takes place when you are daydreaming, zoning out or even meditating. It is the same state that you are in right now because you are reading and same state you are in when you drove home from work but you don't remember doing it because you were thinking about something else. When your brain is in Alpha it is a time when it is extremely receptive yet still conscious. This is important because you want the person to be awake when you are using your Force Powers and applying Force Influence on them because you still have the subconscious accessibility of one who is in a deep trance.

EEG studies have shown that during hypnosis there is a drop in the higher frequency brain waves while simultaneously a rise in lower brain wave activity. These studies reveal that the conscious mind has a tendency to withdrawal while the subconscious mind becomes more active when hypnosis is being applied. This is essential to know if you want to bisect conscious rationalization and employ Force Influence to do the Jedi Mind Trick.

During scientific studies over the years something interesting was reviled. What was discovered was that the left hemisphere of the Brain (the Cerebral Cortex to be

27

exact) becomes less active and the right side becomes more active under hypnosis. As we all know Neurologists have attributed logic and deductive reasoning skills to the left side of the brain and abstract plus emotional reasoning to the right side. With the drastic reduction in activity on the left side of the brain it gives the right side of the brain a stronger influence on a person's decision making skills during hypnosis, thus the mind trick. This is one of the reasons why people are more easily influenced while in other mental states than they are in when they are in Beta.

Understanding brainwaves is just the tip of the iceberg in realizing what is behind the power of The Force and just why Force Influence works. Remember that manifested abilities of The Force are based on the mind therefore our neural makeup is the key to understanding our roll with The Force and is a step in unlocking the secrets of Force Mastery. As new research is found more will be reviled about how we may apply it with use of The Force.

Section 3:

The Method in the Mind Trick?

In general Force Influence works by making use of people's natural instincts to conceptualize by employing specific Force Power techniques called Numinations and also by using habituated cultural norms to induce resourcefulness in the listeners mind. When someone is being resourceful they must reflect on the matter and become slightly distracted because they are putting a good amount of conscious thought into what they are thinking about. While interacting with others it is pretty much impossible for someone to focus all their attention on those interactions when they are simultaneously focusing on conceptualizing. However subconscious attention is always at work and is, as noted earlier, open to your suggestions. It is important that you use your suggestions to mutually keep the listener's conscious distracted while leading the subconscious at the same time. These skills will be thought in depth later in the Numinations section of the book.

Force Influence is a highly unintuitive skill so to become more effective at applying Force Influence it is best to imagine that you are talking to two completely different people at the exact same time, the subconscious person and the conscious person. This will make things much easier for you when employing any Force Sensory technique. Even though conscious and subconscious aspects of thought are part of somebody making up a single identity, both the subconscious mind and the conscious mind, as noted earlier in this chapter, have distinctively separate ways of processing and absorbing perceived information. It is The Force that brings them together and helps create the identity. The Force is the binding element; it is the link that binds us and allows us all to be separate yet one.

Some of the other advantages you will get by using the art of Numinations and speaking to someone on the subconscious level is the ability to take mental shortcuts when communicating with them. Numinations allows you to bypass a good majority of the listener's conscious resistance. It gives you the ability to do this is by taking advantage some of the nuances of regular speech like ambiguity and cultural assumed norms in communication. We will go into this more later on in the book but for now here is and example.

Example:

"Fighting Jawas can cause a scene."

This is just one of the ways you can utilize regular speech and be skillfully ambiguous at the same time. I would like to ask you, what do you think is being said here? Am I saying "if one fights a Jawa it will cause a public incident," or that "two Jawas fighting each other will cause a public incident?" One's interpretation will largely depend on your conditioning and cultural norms, however your subconscious mind cannot decipher between the two interpretations and will actually retain both meanings either way.

What happens is when you are utilizing Numinations and speaking to a subject in a subconscious manner the listeners mind is many times unable to consciously make extensive decisions on how to categorize the meanings being conveyed and will pick certain ones out of habit. It does this because it is often times more effective and because there are lots of categories and sub categories that all information can fit in to. It would take far too much time to consciously organize all that information into all those different sub-categories, so your mind just picks one.

Furthermore using the skill of Numinations to speak to someone on the subconscious level also allows the subjects conscious mind to be active within the conversation while at the same time being unaware of the majority of actual information that is being communicating. This is due to The Forces power to veil of the information you are transmitting to them through the use of Numinaitons.

The way you do this is by communicating what you want to say in a naturally sounding and culturally acceptable style to the listener. While simultaneously activating the listener's brains subconscious associations to the additional meanings and making sure that they are not blatantly obvious to the conscious mind this is key to performing the Jedi Mind Trick. The best ways to do this is to use statements that have an incomplete theme, are ambiguous and have the message you want to send to the listeners' subconscious with in them.

Example:

"I imagine that you can."

As you can see that statement example has an incomplete theme, is ambiguous and has the hidden message of "Imagine that you can." If this is unclear as to how this meets the set conditions after reading the Numinations part of the book you will have a better understanding.

You can also use Force Persuasion techniques to distract the conscious mind by having what you say not fit into any cultural norm at all. This is like a psychological bolt or Psy-Bolt that stuns the conscious mind and puts rationalization into a neurological loop. Kind of like when your computer gets confused on where to look for data. The concept is to overload the listener's normal language processing abilities by having the subconscious mind search for the most appropriate meanings to what ever was said. The subconscious does this by systematically examining the nouns and verbs being used for reference material to compare to past experiences from other conversations. Then unconsciously the mind will swap into position other associated meanings but will lack any true references that pertain to the ongoing conversation.

Example:

"Does that it?"

As you see you after reading this your brain somewhat recognizes the statement but it still makes no sense. That is because the statement is a combination of two culturally accepted statements; "Does that...?" and "Is that it?" yet the statement in and of itself does not fit into any accepted form of speech because it is so ill formed. What this does is make the brain look for the most appropriate answer by using the surrounding communication as a reference. However both meanings will be absorbed into the mind of the listener while also distracting them consciously.

Please be forewarned most subconscious communication is not as ill formed as the previous example that was just an example for that specific technique I chose to make it more obvious to you. Many techniques in Numinations will look and sound like regular grammar in a normal conversation. The syntax error in the last statement is the actual reason why that particular statement works.

To learn more on how to use The Force to communicate subconsciously and perform Force Persuasion you will have to study and become proficient at Numinations. In the Numinations section of the book we will break down the ins and outs on how subconscious communication works and will go into great detail about each specific tool and the aspects on why they are effective.

Section 4:

Purpose in the Trick.

The Force has the uncanny ability to connect with and influence any other living being. By studying the art of Force Influence one will be able to acquire this ability and have subconscious influence over others, conscious perceptions and beliefs.

People's beliefs, cognitions and expectations mold their ability to recognize patterns so they can quantify reality, because of this these thought patterns have a direct influence how we process information. In 2007 Dr. Raz Amir showed in his study the neurological reasons why this is and how a mere suggestion is able to change another person's behavior.

During his study Dr. Raz Amir and his colleagues showed a group of volunteers a visual illusion that could be interpreted in two different ways. The volunteers were given some directions before hand on how to recognize a specific spatial perception about that illusion. After viewing the illusion, the subjects were presented with two buttons both representing one of the potential interpretations of the illusion. The volunteers then were told to press the button that indicated the interpretation of the illusion they felt was the

34

dominant of the two. They conducted this test for both impulsive reactions and also for rationalized intentions. What they discovered was the subjects typically looked for the features in the illusion that they were interested in, and dulled down or even denied anything else.

Using an fMRI (functional magnetic resonance imaging) Raz scanned the volunteers during the study and uncovered something quite remarkable. What Dr. Amir and his Colleagues found out was that there were specific Frontostriatal structures, which included the Dorsolateral prefrontal regions and the Putamen, that were active in selecting which interpretation of the illusion each subject picked.

They found that the Frontostriatal system played an important part when processing the illusions associated biases and its effects on the subjects conflicting visual interpretations. In a sense the subjects were subconsciously searching for evidence associated with the suggested expectations given to them from the original orientation and not objectively processing what they saw at all.

These studies reinforce the notion that the mind filters information by using prior interest, expectations and suggestions. All of this leads to Conformation Bias (which will be discussed in more detail in the next section o the book) and shows us how strong of an influence a subtle suggestion has in influencing that bias.

Section 5:

Force Listening: The Art of Hearing Thoughts.

Force Listening is a Force technique used with Force Persuasion to hear through the use of The Force. With it, a Force Practitioner can come to understand the underlying meaning behind the words in which the speaker chooses as if there was a subconscious language also being simultaneously being spoken when someone speaks.

When people speak they are usually trying to say what they are thinking. When doing so people have a tendency to give off signals to the various ways in which they think, kind of like the infamous Freudian slip. With Force Listening one can pick apart the language to reveal the underlying beliefs, presuppositions, and concerns that the speaker might have about something.

The way this can be done is by listening closely to the choice of verbs being used when the person speaks. Verbs are insightful clues because of the way they equate or not equate to a certain type of sentence. In his book "Stuff of Thought" Steven Pinker shows how verbs tend to have specific groupings based on things like, time, force, space and motion. People in general tend to unconsciously overlook the existence of these specific combinations while simultaneously applying them. This is because while growing up and learning our first language we subconsciously conditioned to these specific types of groupings while learning it.

Verbs seem like they can be grouped into many kinds of meanings, for example, some can be based on things that look similar, sound alike, or maybe feel the same. This is not the actual truth though what their actual groupings reveal is something we as a species naturally and unconsciously have a preoccupation with. Things like how certain states change, the different kinds of motion that exist, or the way energy is applied, and even how we quantify time.

Adjectives are another way people give away how and what they think about things. Pay close attention to the adjectives someone uses it will give you a perspective on the internal workings that influence a persons state of mind and behavior. Take for instance there is a difference between the words long and tall. A mile may be a <u>long</u> way but it is certainly not a <u>tall</u> way, however the antonym of each of them is still short. This shows us as a collective our society gives more value to more expansive things than less expansive or "short" things because we as a culture have taken time to apply them more definitions thus more of our focus. When listening to someone you can also discern the main focus of their thoughts in much the same way.

Words and their rules don't tell us much about the world really but they do tell us a lot about ourselves and how we or one thinks. For example later when you get deeper into this book and begin the study Numinetic Grammar there will be a section called Chronological Tuning, in this section you will learn that participles and tenses can effect the listeners perception of when and where you place something in time when performing a Mind Trick. These same tenses of verbs however also give us direct insight to the speaker's personal view of time as well. So not only does it help you shape their perspective of time but it also lets you know the speakers perspective of time as well. When learning Numinations take this into consideration because it will simultaneously teach you how to use Force Listening while also learning the basics behind Force Persuasion and other Force Sensory powers.

The key to Force Listening is the understanding that one must observe language from a perspective that the verbal communication as just an archaic projection of ones thoughts. It is easy to understand how you can just redefine your perspective so that the many seemingly arbitrary aspects of speech can be viewed now as actual insights into the speakers mind and how they think about things. So when you decide to listen to somebody fully and carefully, then you are hearing not only their words, but also to their feeling on what is being conveyed as well.

In the next section of the book you will be learning how to garner the mystical insights of Force Intuition. Force Intuition is a way to make use of people's inherent psychological misgivings while also giving you an intimate view of their inner mind.

Force Intuition when combined with the art of Force Persuasion becomes a powerful ally to the one who becomes skilled at uniting them. It is your duty to develop and magnify your efficiency at using these great powers together so The Force may grow stronger inside of you.

Chapter 3:

Behind the Shadow of The Force: Force Intuition and

Psychology of the Force.

Section 1:

The Psychology behind the Power of The Force:

Before we start delving in the depths of learning about Force Intuition it is first important that we learn about some psychological misgivings that are inherent to all human beings. These psychological misgivings are a crucial element to how and why Force Sensory powers work and this is why we will be going over them first.

It should be understood that the human brain is not a logical computer, as much as some people would like it to be. It constantly makes judgment errors and calculation errors that stem from Evolution, Cultural oversights and Social Darwinism. In the next part of this book we are going to take an in depth look at some of these psychological misgivings and their value when it comes to their use with Force Powers and most specifically Force Intuition.

Subjective Validation: Subjective validation is when a person psychologically approves something as being correct because it is either meaningful or personally significant to them. This is the reason why it is sometimes called the Personal Validation Effect.

The mistake in rationalization that comes into play with Subjective Validation is when someone perceives two completely separate events and then equates them to a deeper more significant meaning. Sometimes these events or their meanings are linked to a spiritual domain or even a heavenly power. This deeper meaning actually comes from an association to psychologically important events form the perceiver's past and/or dreams. The internal relevancy gives the listener an unusual feeling of connection. This somewhat mystical relationship that is experienced only exists because the person listening has certain expectations, beliefs, and predispositions. This leads them to a Conformation Bias which will be discussed later in the book.

Selective Memory is an intricate as well as the most crucial aspect of Subjective Validation and Force Intuition. Selective Memory is a process of someone choosing favorable confirmation for a memory or focus while at the same time ignoring unfavorable evidence to the contrary. It has been shown in study after study that when a Psychic does a reading on someone, the person listening will focus on the correct assertions by the Psychic and give those assertions more validity than the incorrect assertions. The stronger the desire that person has to believe what is being said, the easier for the Psychic to make vague statements associated to them.

Long before the name Subjective Validation was given to this psychological concept it was called the Forer Effect. The Forer Effect was named after the American psychologist Bertram Forer. Back in 1948 Bertram Forer discovered that people are very susceptible to believing vague depictions about themselves and equating these depictions as distinctive and idiosyncratic of who they are.

In the experiment Forer gave his students a personality test. This test was a fake test because Bertram never even looked at the answers that his students had written. What he did was take a page out of the astrology section of the local paper and then copied it down. Unbeknownst to his students he gave those exact same copies to them as if they were their results. Afterwards Forer asked his students to evaluate the test from 0 to 5, with "5" meaning the student thought the test was an "excellent" evaluation and "0" meaning the assessment was "bad." The class average evaluation was 4.26. This test has now been repeated numerous times all across campuses around the world and the average score still being surprisingly around 4.2 out of 5. The interesting point is that 84% of students keep responding with an overwhelmingly positive reply to the test, with most of the students believing that the study is legitimate and exceptionally accurate at pinpointing their personalities.

As we see, subjective validation is a powerful tool and works because people want to find meaning and give significance to things when sometimes there isn't any meaning or significance at all except the ones we give them in the first place.

It is an evolutionary mechanism that has helped us create religion, writing and art. Some say it is the very mechanism that has led us to become the most dominant species on the planet. Without it there would probably be neither phones nor television, because someone had to believe what they thought could be true without empirical evidence to attest the truth in the first place. Subjective validation is a very powerful component in our psyche and it is the same tool that you will employ using The Force.

Conformation Bias: Confirmation Bias is when someone is selectively looking for or focusing on some kind of validation to support the things that they want to believe while ignoring or devaluing any evidence that could contradict or take away relevancy from that belief. Conformation Bias becomes much stronger when it comes to beliefs based on faith, predispositions and traditions.

The psychological grounds for Conformation Bias seem to stem from the ego. It is notably caused by hope, vanity or our inherent propensity to want to make sense out of things. It creates a tendency for one to interpret facts according to what one wishes to be true rather than what actually is true.

People have a tendency to accept assertions about themselves in proportion to how large their desire is for the statements to be true. People will often not take into account any evidence that is contrary to the desired belief. People will even accept statements that are questionable or even obviously false about themselves, just because they consider them positive and want to believe them. People do this because people deep down don't like to be wrong and anything that shows them that they could be wrong is much harder to accept because of the ego. This is a natural aspect of our psychological evolution and should not be confused as being a sign of unintelligence.

Here is an example, let us say someone wants to believe in telepathy and that I am psychic. That person will consciously focus on when I say things that support their beliefs and take them in as if they were accurate. Now if I were to say something that doesn't fit into their belief then they are likely to forget or relate it to a communication error so it does not impose on their internal belief system. It is the same principal that comes into play when people receive a phone call and they were just thinking about that person. People don't tend to remember all the phone calls that they got when they weren't thinking about that person.

44

People also have emotionally biased beliefs about their self image due to vanity. This leads people to defend these beliefs in a non objective and selective manner. Personal biases tend to get in the way of rational thinking and seem to have a profound effect on ones belief structure. The more emotionally involved the more likely one will ignore facts or empirical data that is contrary. This is because it is much easier and comforting to deal with information that already supports ones belief. It already fits in the person's world view so the information can slip right in without any effort. Although, when it is contradictory information it has a tendency to push one to reevaluate their belief structure for new understandings. This can be taxing and stressful to the mind. So it is much easier to accept statements that already fit in that world view.

It is a very powerful insight to recognize that people have an unconscious tendency to give more significance and credence to information that supports their beliefs than they do to opposing data that doesn't fit their beliefs. It enables you to have extra tools that most will overlook when influencing people.

Ad Hoc Hypothesis: Ad Hoc is a phrase in Latin that means "For this purpose". Typically it is a phrase that suggests a contrived solution designed for problems which come up that refutes the original hypothesis or belief.

Rather than carefully planning a solution that can be used across the board, sometimes people use Ad Hoc Hypotheses to explain away facts that will refute their beliefs as they go along. This is because there has been a psychological gestalt built up within that person and anything to refute this matter will disturb this view point, so they make adjustments to their beliefs to save that beliefs from being falsified, explaining away anomalies that were not anticipated. These explanations may have absolutely no credibility to them what-so-ever but the believer would rather accept these untruths than risk their reality being damaged in slightest. So the sole purpose for what an Ad Hoc is to address immediate problems that arise. This way the person creating the Ad Hoc can protect their beliefs from any opposition even if there is contrary evidence to say otherwise.

Post Hoc: Post Hoc is Latin for "After the fact, therefore because of the fact." This is an informal fallacy that happens when someone thinks that because something happened after an event that something else was caused by the original event. The irrationality in this reasoning is just because two events happened in sequence does not necessarily mean that one has actually caused the other or is even equated to the other. This psychological mistake in reasoning is one of the main elements behind the usefulness of many of the Numonic Grammar techniques later in the book. The Post Hoc error in reasoning is an easy thing to fall into because of its natural chronological aspects. People seem to naturally want to give relevance to the noticeable sequential connections and then relate them to causality. This is far from the truth much of the time. The misleading notion comes from arriving to a conclusion based solely on the order in which the events came by, instead of taking into account other factors that might rule out any seemingly notable connection.

Many superstitions were created because of the Post Hoc fallacy. For instance, there are several athletes that believe that if they don't go through some silly ritual before a game they will lose that game.

The Post Hoc fallacy actually has come from a remarkably useful part of our neurology. What happens is that our neurons get conditioned to do things in sequences because of repetition. This repetition is usually physical or neural. The error is that with Post Hoc, we associate things that aren't necessarily interconnected like our arms and legs. We have learned that if one moves their knee, the leg will raise. After doing this several times we know physically it to be most often true. The Post Hoc fallacy would come in to play when every time you move your knee you notice a plate fall and then associate plates falling with the movement of your knee.

Nevertheless a sequence does not establish credibility in causation. Coincidences happen all of the time and because of the law of large numbers, unbelievable chance occurrences and irrational conclusions will happen. Just because something takes place after an event does not give credence to a connection between the two thus said events. People will always rely on intuition and subjective interpretation and this is why Post Hoc is a helpful tool to utilize.

Section 2:

Force Intuition: Creating the Illusion of Clairvoyance

Cold Reading: Cold Reading is a group of combined skills used by Psychics, Mentalists, and Advertisers to get subjects to behave according to their wishes or believe that the reader has some sort of supernatural powers that allow them to inexplicably know personal details about them or others.   In Cold Reading the reader utilizes people's inherent psychological oversights and realizes that the subject will usually have a propensity to find more meaning in the situation than there really is.

"The Force can have a strong influence on the weak minded".

Obi Wan Kenobi

Our inherent ability to make sense and meaning out of things is an amazing resource that has guided us throughout the ages. Without it, we would not have come up with such great insights such as science, engineering, or even music for that matter. This incredible skill has been the forefront in human evolution and it is the same skill that you will utilize in your future interactions with others; especially when using Force Intuition.

With Force Intuition, there is no need for rehearsed scripts that the Cold Reading psychics use. It works by using The Force and realizing that there are some emotions and life events that are universal and bind us all together. The Force can guide you to certain statements that will have emotionally significant meaning to the listener. These said statements when coupled together create a mysterious wonder inside the listener that psychologically implies an unseen clairvoyance to you.

The first thing you need to understand is that when you are speaking to someone, they will have this tendency to make sense out of whatever you are telling them. People have ego's that are inherently self motivated which leads to a tendency of having overly magnified views about themselves. These tendencies will cause people to be extremely receptive to accepting assertions about the possibilities of what could be. It is also because of these tendencies, that people will ignore or even forget the majority of educated guesses that you will make about them that might be incorrect (unless it attacks their ego), and will remember the ones you will make that are right on the dot (especially if it strokes the ego).

Just knowing the egos effect on people and the psychological oversights that stem from it you can actually do a clairvoyant read on a complete stranger. This ability will create an amazing amount of rapport with them and will allude to you as having some sort of unseen clairvoyant power that will create an intrigue about you, as well as to the conversation, with the listener.

49

Here, let me show you the way. I know I, myself, have never met you personally but I do know that there is an unforeseen psychological bond connecting the both of us simply because you got this book, but it goes well beyond just that. I know that every now and again you seem to be critical of yourself and even though you have some personality flaws you are generally able to compensate for the majority of them. I also know you have a significant yet seldom used talent that you have not yet taken advantage of and that earlier in life you wanted to accomplish something remarkable and very meaningful. Sometimes, you have serious doubts as to whether you have made the right decision or done the right thing. You prefer a specific amount of change and variety and become disgruntled when hampered by restrictions and limitations. Furthermore, I know life's lessons have taught you that it unwise to be overly candid in revealing who you are to others too soon. You also pride yourself as an independent thinker and are not likely to accept another person's assertions without a reasonable amount of proof. You have a clever mind, with a good sense of responsibility and at times, you are extroverted, and sociable, while at other times you are introverted, and reserved. In the year ahead, you will become involved in quite a few new challenging projects. These projects will be loaded with enormous amounts of possibilities. So keep your mind on this and welcome it.

I know that with these statements I may have touched a sensitive part of you, and I do it to show you just how powerful these tools can be. This is Force Intuition in action and is a great skill especially when combined with other Force Powers.

The Illusion of clairvoyance is evident. This is because the human mind is always selectively rationalizing things. The mind can only focus on so much information without having information overload. So people selectively decide what kind of information is worth remembering and how much importance they want to put on it. People do this so they can make sense out of what is happening at the time, but they tend to do it with an undertone of emotional bias. The reason people do this is not because they are gullible or stupid. In fact, it seems to be that a seemingly intelligent person can also succumb to these types of tendencies because of their ability to comprehend abstract thought processes and logically figure out problems. The reason people are privy to this misjudgment tends to be because they just really want certain things to be true and because certain events happen to stimulate specific mental associations.

We know that emotions enhance the feelings associated to remembering. Our memory is predominately controlled by areas of the brain called the Hippocampus and the Amygdala. Studies of the brain have shown decisively that the Hippocampus oversees our memories performance for both neutral and emotional actions whereas the Amygdala has consistently predicted memory performance for only emotional activity. The interesting thing is that the Amygdala systems for arousal seem to have a direct connection with primitive functions such as our survival and reproductive functions. Another unusual trait of the Amygdala is that it is more active with certain emotions than with others. It has been shown in studies that the two limbic areas of the brain, the Anterior Cingulated Cortex and the Amygdala are associated with optimistic viewpoints.

This is important because it gives us proof as to why people tend to be susceptible to conformation bias, and reveals why Force Intuition will work.

In 2004 Tali Sharot, Mauricio R Delgado & Elizabeth A Phelps did a study at New York University that for the first time identified the neural mechanisms that underlined the enhanced feeling of remembering for emotional events. Their studies examining memory have shown convincing evidence that emotions heighten feelings of remembering without actually enhancing the objective accuracy. What they did was show subjects a group of neutral photos and a group of emotion inducing photos. Then they measured each of the subject's brain activity associated with both groups of photos. The subjects then were asked if identification was associated with recalled details or not. For the group of photos that were neutral, the subjects recall was associated with the Parahippocamal Cortex part of the brain; however their subjects recall for the group of emotionally inducing photos created more activity in the Amygdala. This study showed the reason why people rely on emotional arousal and personal ease to evaluate memories.

These neurological tendencies are the root cause for Selective Validation and Conformation Bias (which was discussed earlier in the book), because of the emotional implications of memory. When something strikes a person emotionally the brain reacts by saying says "Hey! Remember this." There are so many instances in life where this has been proven over and over again, your first love, when a parent got mad at you, or even a death of someone close to you.

Section 3:

The Feint - Making Use of Subjective Validation

Manifestations of The Force are mentally-based abilities and tapped through the practitioner's willpower. While performing Force Intuition you will need to have some specific skill sets in your arsenal and one of the most important skills you will need to learn how to do is to create Feint. A Feint is a statement constructed to engage the subject while also narrowing down the field of different possibilities for future statements.

Example:

"I see that you have been thinking about somebody lately." Or

"You have something that you haven't finished and it is really important that you do."

If you notice that neither statement is a question in and of itself. Yet both statements elicit a response from the subject anyway. The Force has an uncanny ability to draw answers from people when a question was not asked. Knowing this you can decide to stack your statements. Stacking works by placing multiple Feints on your subject within one statement amplifies its effectiveness. This is because the subject oftentimes will pay more conscious attention to the Feints that more true than the ones that are not; again, because of Subjective Validation.

Example:

"There is a woman that you have been dealing with that you are not quite seeing eye to eye with. I feel that she is older than you and is a bit reserved in her demeanor."

This technique gives the subject the illusion that you are being very specific, when in fact you are not. Appearing specific when performing a read adds to your credibility in the eyes of the listener, so always look to be viewed as specific. Also when you first start avoid asking a direct question from the subject because it can take away some of the mystique of having telepathic ability. The interesting thing about Feints are that most people become so psychologically engaged trying to find a memory or thought that corresponds to the statement, that they will instinctively issue a response without completely realizing it.

Take note that it is best not to disclose the received information at this point in time, because it is obvious that the information was just reviled. Disclosed information is much more valuable if you can hold it in your memory banks for a while. The reason being is that after a decent amount of time has passed you can summon up the

54

information you have gathered and then recite it like it's an intuitive revelation. Then convey it back to them in a modified form so it seems like it is the first time this information has ever been discussed between the two of you.

Section 4:

The Great Escape

The Force has the ability to influence all living beings. With that being said its influence takes practice to master and another skill you need to have in your arsenal to master The Force is the skill of creating a backdoor for your statements.

Initially in your conversation between you and your subject, its best that you let them understand that your abilities are not always in tune and that your abilities can become unclear at times. If you happen to make a mistake with one of your statements you can easily escape from it by redefining the context or content of the statement. It is important when you make your assertions be artfully vague because to truly understand The Force, you will need contrast and not adhere to a single idea. This makes it easier to redefine the understandings and attribute the oversight to merely miscommunication, (More of this will be discussed later in the book).

Example:

"There is someone with a profound effect on you that is about 5'10"."

The subject at this point will answer your statement with either a positive response or a negative reply. If the subject responds positively flow with it and let them feel like you knew that all along by confirming it.

Example:

Subject "Yes my father! He is 5'10"." Then you say. "Yes, I know."

At the end you may notice the confirmation statement and this will help reinforce the implication that you have psychic abilities while also creating a belief that you were more precise than you actually were.

In contrast, if you receive a negative response to what you said, you now have an out because of the fact that you made the original statement seemingly precise yet artfully vague. This will allow you to change the context or content of your response and now allude to the fact that it was some sort of miscommunication or information distortion that ensued.

Example:

> Subject "No one I know is that tall has and effect on me!" and your
> retort would be something like this. "Maybe not directly but they
> do indirectly. It's possible that they are a friend of one of your
> friends or even a co worker."

This statement diffuses the negation and also retreats the statement to an unknown source that can't actually be verified right away. While taking advantage of Conformation Bias the statement also seeds the subject with something to look for in their future encounters with others, to help prove you are right. It is important that you say your retorts with a lot of conviction because it will lead your subject to more easily believe you. Confidence goes a long way when performing a read on someone.

An important skill you will need to perfect is the art of narrowing down the subjects demographic. This is so you can get especially personal with your subject which grants you the ability to connect with them more and also makes you seem to be telepathic. Each and every person has life experiences that are quite unique to that person; however there are many universal experiences that we all share as well. Theses experiences can be told to almost anybody and will prove to be accurate as well as produce the conformation one seeks when using their Force powers. (You want conformations. They are the key source of narrowing down your subject's personal experiences). Everyone has been sick at one time or another, most people have had an issue with finances at one time or another, and almost everyone has been in love.

Example:

"Do you remember when you were driving your first car? "

There are also certain norms that particular demographics share in their life experiences. Here are a couple of examples, most married women have at some time been suspicious of their husbands, and most young men have wondered weather they will become a success or not. As you see there are universal connectors that certain demographics adhere to. These are very useful in creating a framework to use on your subject.

Example:

"I have a feeling that when you were younger you had a specific interest or subject that you were pretty dedicated to, where you showed a lot of potential. I also get a feeling that this was something on the creative or artistic side, where someone such as your parents may have felt you could have gone on to do great things with it."

As said before, be artfully vague with your assertions when dong a read on someone, because it is in your best interest for accomplishing Force Perception. While you do this it is also best to use generalities that are applicable to large portions of society especially when you are first starting. This is so you can nail the subject down into specific demographics. You can always narrow it down from there.

As you grow and improve in your skills at creating vague statements, you will learn that it is much more efficient to scan your subject for signs that will give you clues so you can make more educated assertions about the subject. This is so you can be much more specific with your statements from the start, which will in turn lead you to be viewed as more intuitive to the subject. Learn to become observant of things, such as the persons accent, clothes, body language, etc. These markers will give off clues as to which demographics your artfully vague assertion can be attributed to. For instance, if you notice someone has calloused hands when you shake it, that is a good sign that they use their hands for some extraneous type of activity, or if someone is wearing a Pinseeker, hat there is a strong likely hood that they or someone they know plays golf. It is important to combine these markers to profile of your subject, and then take note of them so you can make an assertion about it later. It is rather useful to use these fairly commonsense signals to be able to gauge your clients demographic. You will see a big difference in their reactions.

Section 5:

Bounded by Words

The next skill you will want to learn is how to bind your statements. I got this clever concept one morning after watching Katie Couric when she was on the Today Show. What happened was NBC was doing a segment on Dr. Jack Kevorkian, who was known for administrating assisted suicides at the time. At the end of the segment, Katie Couric said something to the extent of "Wow, what a controversial subject, yet not without any merits." When this was said, I felt she was pro assisted suicide and the person I was watching it with thought she said she was against it. At that point I realized she actually didn't make an endorsement of either viewpoint; however at the time both my friend and I certainly thought she had. This led me to realize that you could make a statement sound or seem like you are giving your support to something when you actually are not taking any position what-so-ever. This method is called binding your statements.

"You're going to find that many of the truths we cling to

depend greatly on our point of view".

Obi Wan Kenobi

Binding your statements is the concept I created to be more specific without having to commit to anything in particular that you have just said. A bounded statement is one that will credit the subject with having elements of a specific personality trait and the direct opposite trait as well. It works by employing the effect of Confirmation bias and Subjective Validation. What it does, is it creates no out in your statement so you will always be perceived as being right, even if you have absolutely no clue.

Example:

"In general you are a good person, although you do have a bad streak that can come into play at times."

If you notice in the statement, the subject is called both good and bad at the same time. This causes Subjective Validation to jump in and pick the stronger belief of the two then focus on that.

These statements are fairly simple to create. What you want to do is consider any common personality trait and then describe that trait and the exact opposite trait in the same statement. You can also say they have and lack thus said trait as well, however it is not that important so long as you bind the statement by covering both bases. It is important that when you do this you want to avoid making any statements where the personality trait is associated to something that is obviously quantifiable like another person or work it has the capability of failing. Keep your statements to the subjective non tangible realm of things. It will make things a good deal easier and you will have much greater success. Now, after you have done all of this, connect your personality traits up with a sub-statement that doesn't dismiss the original personality trait.

Example:

"yet in certain situations" or "at times" and "you also have the potential to".

Notice how the sub-statement does not take anything away from the originally stated personality trait.

Binds work because people's emotions are not static. Emotions are fluid and are changing all the time, and because of this, bounded statements are almost always correct. The surprising outcome of a bounded statement is that it gives off an effect of emotional insightfulness which in turn helps you bypass walls and helps you create an astonishing amount of rapport with the listener.

This next type of bind has a completely different kind of effect than the binds you have just learned to do, but it is just as practical and can be used in a variety of circumstances. The way it works is to use a positive and a negative in the same sentence when posing a question. This is so you can come off as already having some insight and are just looking for a little confirmation.

Example:

> "I know you have been reading this book, you don't like reading this do you?" (Note: Inflection is important here so keep it as neutral as possible.) If the answer is positive "Yea I do!" you say something to confirm their answer such as, "I thought so." If the answer is negative "Nope, don't like it." you can reply, "I didn't think so."

The reason this works is because the brain has an interesting way of computing a negative statement. It will process the statement first without the negation so it is able to acknowledge what is being negated, and then it handles negating it afterwards. So all you are to do is confirm what ever they say, and the brain in general will accept it. This becomes even more powerful if you expand upon your agreement with the subject, because it helps them forget about the subtle misstep.

Example:

> "I thought so because…" or "I didn't think so since…"

> *"So what I told you was true… from a certain point of view".*
>
> *Obi Wan Kenobi*

Because we are on the topic of using opposites, I feel it is a good time to explain an aspect of creating a good Feint. One aspect is to suggest that there is someone in the subject's life that the subject doesn't get along with. When doing this simply describe the person that the subject doesn't get along with, by using personal attributes that are the direct opposite of your subjects. In general there is always someone that your subject won't get along with and there is a high likelihood of them having some opposite characteristic traits. The technique in a sense uses the opposite effect of Subjective Validation combined with Confirmation Bias because they don't want to be related to the person they don't like.

Example:

> "I get a feeling that there is a person at your work that you don't
> get along with very much. They seem to take situations a little too
> seriously and can't seem to leave things alone when dealing with
> matters that don't concern them."

A major key to the success of a mind read is the subject's willingness, effort, and capability to find meaning and significance in what your have told them. The odds are in you favor that the subject will find meaning because of their own neural susceptibility to Subjective Validation and Confirmation Bias. Be confident in your assertions or predictions even if they are wrong, many times the subject will recall some memory where it applies anyway, especially when given a little assistance from you.

Watch for feedback from your subject; whether it is verbal or non verbal. You can use this feedback to gauge the subject on how much they agree or disagree with your statements. You can use it as a basis for the direction of the conversation and for the use of empathy. Most importantly you are able to use the subject's feedback to reveal value contradictions between what the subject says and what the subject really believes. People will not always be honest and you want to be able to detect it whenever possible.

Lastly you want to do a recap to your subject of all of your hits just as a reminder before you or they leave. This will allow them time to focus on all of the assertions that went well for them. Like we said earlier in the book emotions have a direct link to memory. So, focus on the positive successes with your affirmations and the mistakes will later vanish with time. Enjoy using this technique and be chivalrous with your endeavors. These skills are to gather insights and understandings to better gain rapport; not to manipulate others. I say this with an extremely strong emphasis. For The Force is one's ally and it is only through interaction through decision, integrity, and through mental and physical effort, that The Force can grow with inside ones being.

Chapter 4:

Numinations: The Language of The Force

Section 1:

Numination: The Act of Subconscious Communication:

The Force is believed to reside in a person's mind and feelings, and it is understood that knowing The Force will allow one to peer into the feelings hidden inside the minds of others. One must have the patience and dedication to condition this sensitivity so one may truly understand the power and nature of The Force.

In this section of the book you will be learning basic elements on how Force Sensory powers work. Some of the chapters may seem more like academia but with practice you will learn to better understand its unique connection to The Force.

Numination: Numination is a word I created to define a method of communicating subconscious thought from one person to another. It is derived from the concept of being numinous – which refers to the ability to communicate thoughts and/or actions in a telepathic way, through a sort of supernatural connection of minds. However there is no real magical element to this form of communication, this form of communication is part of The Force and depends solely on people's involuntary reactions, unconscious information gathering and conditioned responses that have been habituated into their subconscious minds. Numinations is the key to having success in mastering your Force Sense abilities. This is because Numination is the method that channels The Force so you can consciously influence your intuition and it is also a way of teaching yourself how to observe unconscious reactions in others, both of which are vital elements to your understanding of Force Sense abilities.

What would you to say if I were to tell you that the majority of the knowledge that you hold is in all actuality outside the sphere of your own conscious awareness? Would you believe me? Well believe it or not The Force is all around us at all times and there is in fact a bounty of unrealized information stored someplace in your mind, and that place is called your subconscious mind and that knowledge is referred to as "Tactic Knowledge or Implicit Knowledge." When creating a connection with The Force we can access this knowledge and use it for our own good and for the good of others.

Tactic Knowledge is an element in all of The Force. You may not know this but Tactic Knowledge is all the information that your brain has made systematic to make things more effective and easier for you. This is so that when you've performed a certain task or action a specific amount of times it will take little or no conscious effort to perform this action over and over again. "It's just like riding a bike." as the saying goes. These actions and/or thoughts now become totally integrated in the brain and then automatically occur. It as if your brain is programming its self. This underlying process that is taking place is the power of The Force working through us so we do not have to do these things.

> *"What we think of as free will is largely an illusion: much*
> *of the time, we are simply operating on automatic pilot,*
> *and the way we think and act are a lot more susceptible to*
> *outside influences than we realize.."*
>
> *Malcom Gladwell*

Section 2:

Monkey See Monkey Do

What if I were to tell you one does not even have to perform the action or task for The Force to activate those specific receptors in the brain. People indeed can also gain Tactic Knowledge by just watching an action in and of it's self. Taking note of the latest discoveries in Mirror Neurons (a specialized type of Neuron) and how they function, certain scientific studies have shown with out a doubt that this is actually what is happening inside us all the time.

A little over a decade ago a man named Dr. Giacomo Rizzolatti and a group of neuroscientist at the University of Parma had stumbled upon some incredible events while researching some macaque monkeys and how their brains function. What Dr. Rizzolatti and his group of scientists discovered was that pre-motor neurons within these monkeys brains were working when the macaques performed a task that was goal based, like grasping objects, and also, more importantly, when the saw other monkeys doing the same things. During these experiments they simultaneously discovered that those same brain cells in the macaques were being set into motion also when they were watching a human doing certain goal based tasks as well.

As revolutionary as Dr. Rizzolatt's study has been it has merely opened the door to the numerous amounts of possibilities for what the brain can do. Modern research now shows us that people also have these nifty little mirror neurons working inside us as well and the amounts are even more numerous, are much better at adapting and are far more evolved than any of the neurons found in the macaques or any other type of monkey for that matter. Scientists reason that this must be a direct reflection of the evolution of the human species and why we have such advanced social abilities and I believe that with the power behind Numinations our brains will advance even more.

Most of the nerve cells in a persons brain are pretty much ordinary, however modern research has found that the human brain has a multitude of Mirror Neurological systems that essentially specialize in understanding and employing not only ones actions but also ones intentions as well. This is important because it is a key factor for why Numinations works.

"Mirror neurons allow us to grasp the minds of others not through conceptual reasoning but through direct simulation."

Dr. Giacomo Rizzolatti

During Dr Rizzolatti studies he showed that if one were to reach for a glass while someone else was watching, the watcher's exact same neurons would fire as the one performing the action in and of it self (just like the Monkeys). The interesting thing is

70

that this phenomenon was not limited to just sight it applied to other senses as well. When one listened and heard a specific action take place or even saw the action being related to a specific sound, the same neurons would again fire.

So when you see someone performing an action your brain actually simulates that exact same action which then creates a stencil or guide for you to use to recreate that action for yourself. Studies have shown that these same templates are what allow us to read the intentions of others because they give us the ability to predict what other people will do next. For example if you see a quarterback bring his arm back with the football in his hand you have a good instinctive possibility that he is going to throw it or at least try to.

Knowing Numinations is an important ability because it connects with The Force through the listeners Tactic Knowledge while utilizing preconditioned responses and mirrored neurological stimulus for a result. Because of this you will find using Numination extraordinary useful. You will discover that it can be used to consciously direct peoples thoughts and feelings, which will give you the ability to use Force Persuasion on others. It gives you the ability to create Force Intuition by condition yourself to read others nonverbal cues so clearly that you will pretty much be able to read their minds. With these skills in The Force you will be able to eliminate conflict when exchanging ideas, cut learning times to a minimum by evoking Force Comprehension and use The Force to establish an exceptionally strong rapport with people that usually takes years or a few emotionally powerful experiences to create. Numination is the tool that will endow you with the capability to do all this and more.

Numination is broken down into two distinct areas of learning. The first is Numonics (associated to Force Persuasion and Force Intuition) which has to do with the use of audible and.sometimes written language in subconscious communication and the other is Numinetics (Associated with Force Intuition, Precognition and Telepathy) which has to do with the nonverbal aspects of communication and the body's way of communication subconscious information. With these two exceedingly powerful skills you will be able to see the world in a brand new light and have an unlimited amount of possibilities right at your fingertips. Practice these skills, learn them well and then you will command the power of The Force.

Section 3:

The Numonic Lexicon: Vocabulary of The Force

This section of the book is about the Numonic Lexicon and its use for embedding commands within Force Sensory Powers.

What would you say if I told you that the words you commonly use now have a profound effect upon others you speak to? A magical underlying effect that is more powerful that one could ever imagine. An effect that can guide peoples thoughts to a predestined conclusion through your own will. You may think that I am not telling you the truth or you might be skeptical to the amount of influence your words truly have. However with The Force as your ally you can use it and channel it through your words.

Your words do have power and do have the influence to guide others. As proof one of the worlds leading psychologists in automatic influences on human behavior and free will, John Bargh, reviled that people were profoundly influenced, unconsciously, by very simplistic things like words.

In one of his many automatic human behavior experiments John Bargh had some of his students watch an on screen a series of flashing words in what is called a "Scrambled Sentence Test." These words that flashed upon the screen were very specific so he can see how these selected words might influence and condition the viewer's minds. The first group of students was given a list of fifteen words that were associated with negativity and being rude, words such as disturb and annoying. Conversely the second group of students was shown a completely different set of words upon the screen. These words were positive words associated with respect and courtesy, words like polite and appreciate. The third and last group of students was given a list of fifteen traditionally neutral words that had no relation to any kind of social etiquette what so ever. After putting the different groups of students through their specific word conditioning John Bargh manufactured an event afterwards that might influence the students to act accordingly to their recent conditioning, either rudely or politely. After the experiments were finished he gathered and studied the information. During his examination he noticed that the students had overwhelmingly acted in accordance to their conditioning earlier that day. The students conditioned with the polite words acted politely and the students conditioned with the rude words acted rudely.

The study showed just how easily the unconscious mind is influenced by mere words alone and this reaction was only after a few minuets of being shown specific words. What if you could do that yet with even more control? Here let me explain more.

As revealed earlier the brain is shown to unwittingly act according to its socialization and because of this we have grouped together a series of useful words that some professionals in the fields of hypnotherapy and mentalism use to direct influence upon their clients or audience members. These words are Force inspired and will be the basis for what you are about to learn. They are the foundation for your use of Force Influence and Force Intuition. With these building blocks you can understand how to break down and organize the techniques of Numinations thus utilizing the power that is The Force. This is the Numonic Lexicon and it is powered by The Force.

Lexicon (lek-si-kon, -kuh n): The vocabulary of a particular language, field, social class, person, etc.

Lexicons are very useful because they give a certain amount of credibility to their particular fields of study. They also give us the ability to better communicate our disciplines categories of related information, categories that may not be used normally in another discipline or other form of study. This comes quite in handy when communicating with others in the field and eliminates time wasted explaining matters over and over again each time you want to use a certain skill set.

As opposed to a more regular lexicon, the words within The Force channeling Numonic Lexicon have a sub-list of words within it. Each of those words in the sub-lists of our Numonic Lexicon has a subliminal like effect on the listener's unconscious mind (As spoke about it the Jedi Mind Trick Chapter) because they have socially conditioned associations to other related thoughts. This is vital to the foundation of learning Numinations because it is a building block for learning the Numonic Grammar techniques that move and direct the power of The Force.

Actuators: (A): (Examples: can, would, might, should, must, ought, and will.) These are merely action words. Actuators are useful especially with Force Persuasion because they are commands that when spoken create a predictable thought or actualization within the listeners mind. It is important that you realize that the actuators may or may not create the action in and of its self, but they will through presupposition create the thought of that said action.

Example:

"You can read as much as you like"

Now as you see you may not want to read more but your mind went over the thought of reading more nevertheless. Use these Actuators and combine them with some of the other techniques in this book to get the most optimal use out of them.

Bridge (B): (Examples: But, However, Although, Nevertheless, Nonetheless, Except.) Are words and phrases related to negations (see: negations) that "bridge" the negated idea to a seeming similar idea to imply a misunderstanding by the listener. A bridge must be use with tact because you want the listener to only know there was a miscommunication between the two of you, not an implication that the listener was wrong, even if they were.

Confirmations (YS): (Examples: Yes, Of Course, Sure, Good, Okay, Yea, That's Right.) Conformations are the use of words and/or phrases to affirm to the conscious mind that you understand what is being said to you. Simultaneously these Conformations give subconscious praise to the subjects mind for following directions that you give to them.

Conformations work by using the same principals that the Pavlovian response uses. This is by giving a socially conditioned response of praise to a subject so that your subject is more likely to stick to the new thoughts and/or conditions given to them.

Example:

"Of course you like what you have learned so far in this book."

Commands (Cmd): (Examples: Now, Stop, Will, Expect, ALL Inductions.) Commands are words that have an immediate impact on the listener. These are some of the most powerful words used in the Numonic lexicon and some of the most intrusive as well. Use them sparingly for you will come off as brash and overly forward if you use them too frequently.

Example:

"Now, it's time for you to stop and think about this."

Chronological (Ch): (Examples: Before, Soon, Now, Then, During, Eventually Prior and After.) These are words that utilize some aspect of time and/or number sequence. Chronological words can be used is to place certain thoughts into certain chronological orders or in different times within the mind of the listener.

Example:

"You probably want to take care of that real soon"

The statement above puts the thought of action close to the present as well as somewhat in the near future.

Example:

"You probably want to take care of that after your trip"

This statement, however similar, puts the same thought of action distinctively further in the future than the first statement. It as if you are planting seeds in the mind of your subject to imagine specific time references. (Chronos Studies)

Another aspect where Chorological words can be used is to provide an illusion of conscious choice when the listener is making a decision.

Example:

"Would you like to practice before or after eight o'clock?"

The listener will generally consider the two options and make a conscious decision. However the listener typically tends to overlook the fact that they are subconsciously conceding to the act of practicing nevertheless. More on this will be covered later in the book.

Inductions (Ind):   (Examples: Imagine, Wonder, Consider, Suppose, Realize, Assume) Inductions are used to induce a slight trance in the listener. Inducing trance puts the users mind in a passive state.   Some are the same as Realizers:

Example:

"Let's suppose you will actually take the class."

You also may use an Induction word in the first person if you feel the listener knows what you are doing, and you do not want to be so obvious about the induction.

Example:

"I wonder what taking this class will be like."

Notice how the brain reacts in a similar way to each of the sentences. You may find one of the statements to be stronger for you than the other or both the same. It will vary amongst different people. Find out which one works best for different circumstances and with practice you will become extremely proficient at using it.

Link (LK): (Examples: And, Plus, In Addition, Furthermore, Also, Because, Moreover, As Well As.) A link is a word that links two thoughts and/or ideas together without negating the previous thought and/or idea. This can be used to create a post hoc or ad hoc rationality within the listener.

Example:

"You like what you have learned so far and you seem like you want to learn even more."

The fist thought most likely is true or you would not have read this much so far never the less that does not equate to the second thought in the statement to be true, yet it sets up a precedence for it to become true in the mind of the listener.

Negations (Neg): (Examples: No, Never, Not,) This is used to deny or nullify a listeners idea. Negs are quite weak if used in a more forward manner because of the brains inner workings. To negate something, something must already exist at least as an idea. So be careful because you do not want to boorishly contradict anything in the listener's internal experience. However they are quite useful when use covertly.

It's important to make sure you understand that a thought has to be in the mind of the listener first and foremost to be able to negate it, this in and of itself can make Negs useful. This is because you can apply Negs as reverse psychology to the listener, and why you can use the Neg covertly.

Example:

"Not now."

When saying "not now" the mind jumps right to now by firstly unconsciously ignoring the "not" and proceeding to now and then negating the "now" afterwards. So it is actually absorbed in the mind more like "now, not."

Also Negs can be used to cover your tracks at times as we know two negatives make a positive. Try to apply this technique when someone is a bit stubborn or you want to hide the direction you are moving the person to.

Example:

"That is not, not what I am saying either."

If you notice this makes the brain confused or a bit which makes it useful when using Force Persuasion.

Nominalizations (NZ): (Non-tangible nouns) (Examples: Feelings, Thought, Love, Emotions, Curiosity,) Nominalizations are nouns that are not a person place or thing. Some Nominalizations tend to be a link between Rational Logic and Dream Logic because they are simultaneously both a process word and noun. Nominalizations effectiveness comes from the fact that they are vague and allow the listener to search their own mind for meanings that best suit there internal representations because of this Nominalizations are a crucial element when using Force Intuition.

The use Nominalizations are very beneficial in working with Force Sensory powers because you can give commands or express certain insights to the listener without risking saying something that contradicts anything in their internal experience.

Example:

"I know there are certain thoughts that you might be thinking right now."

As we can see in this statement the words thoughts are really ambiguous in this statement. This vagueness helps induce the listeners subjective validation just so they can make some kind of meaning to the statement.

Noncommittals (NC): (Examples: Probably, Have a tendency, Possibly, Maybe, Often, Can, Usually, Sometimes, Likely, Tends to, At times.) A phrase and/or statement where one is able to cover certain criteria within that said statement without having to commit entirely to the statement in and of itself. Noncommittals induce Subjective Validation within the listener and are a great why to create Force Intuitive statements for them as well.

Example:

"I realize sometimes you might feel as if this could be something you might do."

Noncommittals are versatile because of their inherent ability to let the listener pick what they want to hear from what is being said, without you having to commit yourself to the statement in and of itself.

Realizers (R): (Examples: Imagine, Realize, Aware, Recognize, Notice, and, Identify.)A phrase or statement that will bring a thought or an idea into realization within the person you are speaking to. Realizers are very good to use for inducing trance.

Example:

"I imagine that certain thoughts might be running through your head right now."

What happens when you use a Realizer is that it brings that thought to the foreground of the listeners mind and gives you the ability to guide it. Realizers are amazing tools and can be used in Force Persuasion as well as with Force Intution.

Spatial (SP): (Examples: Among, Beyond, Inside, Within, Outside, Surrounded.)These words create a correlation between two things. This is so you can put thoughts in a relative area within the listeners mind.

Example:

"Inside I know you know this to be true."

In this same statement if I were to say outside instead of inside the listener would not associate to the statement and more likely disassociate from it.

Spice (Adverbs/Adjectives): Is the act of putting words that describe things in front of any noun you wish to use. This action unconsciously forces the listener to use their imagination. When you use a lot of Spice the listener will often times go into trance by the mere use of the spice in and of it's self, which makes it useful for Force Persuasion.

This works in the same manner as when you have a friend that explains every single detail about a situation and you start to ignore them and passively listen to them. Believe it or not during this passive listening state you are susceptible to suggestions made by the person speaking about their situation.

Section 4:

Numonic Grammar: The Syntax and The Force:

When using the Jedi Mind Trick just using any command on the listener will not do. Not many people are going to listen to you if you are just going around barking orders at them. There is an actual "trick" to how The Force works and how you have to use it to be effective when speaking to them. There is a certain way you have to word things that create that magical control over their mind without them knowing it. It is the Numonic Grammar and it is the language of The Force.

The Language of The Force may sound and seem like the language you are now using but there are unique rules that apply to it that are undoubtedly different. In this next section we are going to go over the Numonic Grammar it is the rules of language when using The Force. Numonic Grammar is applied for any Force power that has any type of speaking involved.

Introductory Force Flow:

Force Flow is the use of words to maneuver your target to a selected mindset. It does this by using a persons conditioned associations of criteria that are related to specific thoughts or ideas. It is a very complicated and a highly advanced procedure that cannot be covered effectively with in the limits of this chapter and most likely would need a book unto itself.

However we will go over a few techniques associated to Force Flow to help start things in the right direction.

(X>Y) A basic key to Force Flow is to equate words and phrases so they contain a hidden impressions within them. People tend to overlook these impressions and actualize them as truths because of ad hoc or post hoc rationalizations. This is extremely valuable in suggesting, asserting, influencing and directing anyone you wish to talk to.

1) Opportunistic: These are statements or questions that utilize everything a speaker says to ones advantage. It is useful because it makes the original speaker reflect and change their focus onto their perceptions of the matter instead of the external happenings at the time.

When employing an Opportunistic statement you will convey what the speaker has said by making use of key words in the said statement but redirecting them to a different outcome. It is great for causing doubt shock or even confusion about what the speaker's beliefs regarding what they had just said.

Example:

Speaker "This stuff doesn't work." You "That is right it doesn't work. That's because you haven't figured out the right way of how to use it yet."

As you can see Opportunistic statements can be a bit intrusive. So make sure you have created a positive relationship with the person that you use them on or just be extremely tactful when employing them.

This leads us to the Opportunistic question which I find to be a stronger tactic and one I like to use more often to loosen someone rigid beliefs or viewpoints. An Opportunistic question is a question made as though one has already preconceived the speakers answer and already has a direct insight about it.

Example:

Speaker "Having that kind of power would be great." You "Exactly what is it about the power that will make it great?"

This technique is good to use for people who are stubborn and you want to loosen them up so they are more able to absorb information when performing Force Persuasion. It addresses their beliefs and makes the listener reflexive.

88

2) Groundless Equations: $(X=/=Y)$ Equating two things together that don't necessarily belong together to make use of Post hoc and Ad hoc rationalizations. This is when you are going to attribute certain happenings to a predefined cause that may or may not have anything to do with the original event.

One of the major flaws in reasoning with even the most rational of minds is to perceive links of a relationship between two things when many times one does not exist. Everyday people have this tendency to quantify things and irrationally make connections between seemingly unrelated occurrences. This happens because the mind has an instinctive ability to seek order amongst the midst of chaos. Most minds dislike chaos so much that they will retreat from rationality into irrationality if that is the only way to make something understandable. Thus, when two or more events happen relatively close together, many people will construct elaborate causal links using Ad-hoc Post-hoc reasoning between them just because of our natural instinct to quantify.

The Groundless Equation technique causes the subject to accept preconceived resolutions more easily and without as much trepidation by the employing the innate selective validation within the listener psyche.

Using a linking word while employing this technique creates a certain strength or credibility to the next statement you would make even though they may have nothing to do with one another.

Example:

"You are reading at these pages because it is the best thing you can

do for your own personal growth."

You may also use Noncommittals to express the effect you wish to have the listener accept.

Example:

"As you read this you might think to your self about how many

ways you can use this."

The third way of using this technique is to use an Actuator and this is the most effective way of implementing this technique.

Example:

"The mere act of scanning these words will make you a much

better communicator in the end."

If you notice there is a common theme with the all of the examples that were given. The common theme is that they all use immediate occurrences and associate them to desired outcomes. The reason this technique works so efficiently is because implies that the original occurrence somehow makes something else happen ie: post hoc. It does this in such a gradual fashion that the listener is taken off guard and will not be as stubborn or inflexible as they might be if they knew what you were doing.

3) Deleted Association: The act of equating something to naught (X=0). This is a non-existing correlation or an association to nothing what so ever. In this technique the object or one of the subjects of the sentence is totally missing. While employing the effect of selective validation this technique makes the listener naturally want to fill in the blanks to what is missing in the sentence. The great thing about this is the artfully vagueness of it. The listener fills in the blanks and supposes you knew what that blank was in the first place. This gives off the illusion of you having some personal insight to their innermost thoughts and in turn creates an incredible psychological bond.

Example:

"I know that you are interested." or "And it is pretty useful….."

This is a great technique when employing Force Intuition. You now may be beginning to notice how important subjective validation and conformation bias is to using Force Intuition this is just the tip of the ice berg. As you delve deeper in your Force training you will find that there is much more to be reviled on its effectiveness.

Conjection:

Conjection is the art of Conjuring up explanations or ideas in the mind of the listener by the use of that person's cultural, educational, and neurological habituation.

Because people have become accustom to doing things a certain way they create neurological bonds in their mind and nervous system that automates these things for efficiency reasons. Conjection takes these patterns and utilizes them to direct the listener to specific thought patterns.

a) Presuppositions: Assuming something: The act of implying ideas in a topic by making use of culturally inherent outcomes.

b) Phantom Nouns: Sometimes you may want someone who is listening to you to think of something specific but it is inconvenient or just plain not in your best interest to say what that is. A useful way to avoid having to say what it is and have the listener think of it for them selves is to say something with the elements that the specific focus has. A great way to do this is to delete the noun related to it in the first place. Anything that is said with an action word in it presumes something performed the action, ergo all verbs presume a preceding and/or following noun. This will allow the listener to fill in the blanks for themselves by using post hoc rationalization.

Using this knowledge you can create or implant the concept of something existing inside your subjects mind with out ever mentioning it. However it is best to use a verb associated to the noun you wish the subject to think about.

Example:

"He pulled the trigger"

In this statement we never make reference to a finger however in the minds of most people a finger or even a hand is presumed. The reason for this is because we have social conditioned responses that relate a finger to a pulled trigger. The great thing about this is that we didn't even make reference to a gun a trigger could be on a water bottle and yet most, even though a lesser number of people, will also assume the gun in their mind.

c) Negated Existence: When something is negated while communicating with others it is truly impossible to subconsciously negate that particular detail altogether. This is true because one must quantify the existence of something before they can consciously negate that very same existence.

Example:

"Don't think of a purple watermelon."

In this statement you must first think of the purple watermelon before you can negate it. The mere mention of it creates the thought within the listeners mind. If the thought did not exist you would not have to negate it.

d) Sequential: This is when one uses some kind of measure on a topic that infers there are either previous or forthcoming topics associated with it.

For example if I were to tell you that the third man on the bench had just left. There is an implicate understanding that there were two more men on that same bench that the man that had just left was on.

Sequential presumptions are not only limited to numerical measures. They exist as a subset in any Chronological communication (see Chronos & Chronological)

e) Mindreads: This is the act of claiming to know the thoughts and/or feelings of someone else without giving any specifics on the method by which you came to know this information by.

Example:

"You may wonder just how this is working" or "Some of these techniques create a certain curiosity inside of you."

This type of approach is an effective way to create mystical credibility in the eyes of the listener. It is important that when you make a mind reading statement that you keep it vague. This is because if it is too specific you run a risk of saying something counter to what the listener is experiencing and in doing so you loose the credibility that you wished to gain in the first place. This is a very powerful adaptable method of creating psychic credibility to the listener and also a great technique to use with Force Intuition and Force Persuasion.

As you can see Conjection utilizes a persons conditioning whether it be social or cultural. Conjection allows you to direct a person to think what you want them to think by inferring the thought itself. The greatest part about it is that the subject will believe they are thinking for themselves.

Elusive Intention:

Audio Illusions: Are key techniques that utilize the inherent processing nature of the subconscious mind and as we have learned earlier the subconscious has a direct connection to Force Powers. Audio Illusions are best used with Force Persuasion because they are hidden messages that you want to embed in the listener to help guide their subconscious mind.

The subconscious mind has a tendency to associate things that have similarities to one another. The similarities may not be consciously rational nevertheless the subconscious mind does arrange them into its own types of classifications. Let me give you an example; the number four can be associated with a car to your subconscious mind because most cars have four wheels and many have four doors. Most people have learned to associate cars with having four wheels because their first observation of a car. These seemingly illogical (they are not really illogical just dream logic) associations are made quite frequently to make processing information less complicated for us. Because of this one can use sounds that are similar to give the subconscious mind variant meanings to what is being said. This gives one the ability to implant hidden messages within the structure of the language being used on the subject.

Variable Expressions: Variable Expressions consist of two unique types of

96

words in the English language one being homophones and the other homonyms. Homophones are words that sound the same, have various meanings and can be spelled differently, such as the words; Vein, Vane, and Vain.

There are also words that are pronounced and spelled the same yet have multiple definitions called Homonyms such as; Patients- One who receives medical attention, care, or treatment, or Patients- Capable of calmly awaiting an outcome or result; not hasty or impulsive. The reason these are important is because they give you the ability to veil a separate message within your communications with others.

The breakdown of how you may use this is first you need to figure out what message you want to embed into the recipient's subconscious. Then make a mental list of all the words you wish to involve in the message. Check each word and its synonyms to see if there are any that have homonyms or are homophones. Now you want to utilize the new indistinct words in a type of shell sentence or wrapper emphasizing the word or words you have chosen

Example:

Wait here (hear) is what I am saying.

In this example we are subconsciously telling the listener to hear as in take note to what is being said. This works especially well if you also emphasize the other words that are in the subconscious command (what I am saying). You may also notice that this has much more of a profound effect on the brain than just the statement "wait here". That is because the "Hear what I am saying" part of the statement is focusing on the listener's ability to pay attention.

Phrase Distortions :   Similar to the homophone is phrase distortion or mondegreen. A phrase distortions are a string of words that result in a mishearing or misinterpretation of a statement like; Youth in Asia as to Euthanasia. To create a Phrase Distortion one should simply apply phonetically hidden words to a word to create the Audio Illusion for example; Trace-formations can be said as Transformations. You may also want to equate two phrases that sound the same to create a Phrase Distortion such as Ice cream, I Scream, or Eye Scream.

Example:

"Come look at the sky." can be phonetically changed to "Come look at this guy?"

By purposefully slurring words or eliminating specific sounds one can create a plethora of fun and interesting Phrase Distortions. Come up with your some of your own Phrase Distortions and share them with others that are great to use with Force Persuasion.

Punctuation Distortion: A Punctuation Distortion is similar to a Phrase

Distortion however it is the act of hiding a sentence within other sentences by either misstating punctuation or not using any at all. William S. Burroughs did this often when writing and it is where I got the idea.

>Example:
>"Did you see that team Win? The game you play tomorrow will be exactly like that."

The two main statements are first the question "Did you see that team win?" The second statement is "The game you play tomorrow will be like that." However there is a third hidden statement with in these two statements and that is "Win the game you play tomorrow." ("Did you see that team Win? The game you play tomorrow will be exactly like that.")

An easy way for you to do this is to look for a Variable Expression that you can use at the beginning of a sentence and at the end of a sentence. Take for example the word hand. Make the sentence with the Variable Expression on the end of it (You have a strong hand.) mentally delete the Variable Expression (you have a strong…) audibly connect it to a sentence with the same Variable Expression in the beginning of it (Hand that to me.) Then add what you need to make the sentence coherent to the listener. (You have a strong *Hand, that to me* could be an asset.)

This is very useful while using Force Persuasion to hide commands within ones conversation without the listener being consciously aware of it. The tactic is somewhat like subliminal man from the old Saturday Night Live television show but far less obvious or invasive. Keep in mind the illusions work best when combined with other Force Sensory skills or with multiple embedding techniques.

Syntax Veil: Syntax Veils depend highly upon cultural norms because of the common accepted comprehension of the specific outcome in certain statements. There are statements though that are not well formed that could have two different outcomes for instance; "Use your common sense for a change." As you can see grammatically this is not a well formed sentence because it can be understood in two entirely different yet distinctive ways.

The first way one might comprehend this statement is that the person being spoken to might not be using their common sense. On the other hand there is a second idea being conveyed in the statement. It is that one must use their common sense to produce a change

Like all Audio Illusions the subconscious brain does not differentiate between the two different meanings in a Syntax Veil like the conscious mind does. This is useful while using Force Persuasion and you want to implant some thoughts or ideas into your subjects mind without them knowing it. It conceals your messages and looks as if you are speaking with normal candor to your subject.

An easy guide to make your own Syntax Veils is take a verb add the letters (ing) to it and then a noun. As in. "Running horses can cause injury." To whom, the horses or to the person who is running them? There are many other ways you can make your own Syntax Veils however this is a great method to get you accustomed to doing so. After some practice you will find ways that suit your style best so you can become more effective at using Force Persuasion.

Missing Reference:

Unknown Originator: Stating an aspect about something without having any specification to the noun associated with that aspect. With this technique the listener is unaware of what the noun associated to the statement will be and therefore will go back using conformation bias and search within their mind to make the sentence make sense to them.

Statements using an Unknown Originator are particularly effective because they have a way of subconsciously slipping in commands to the listener. This is because there is no true reference point and typically the subconscious will accept both messages as the same time. This action will also lead the listener to consciously supply the originator of the action just for the statement to make sense to them. That is why it is important to be observant of peoples conformation bias.

Example:

One is able, to use The Force." In this example there is no concrete evidence for knowing exactly who the person described as one is.

Example2:

"It's good to use The Force." In this statement there is no reference to who exactly is making that judgment.

To create your own Unknown Originator statements just start out by making a accurately constructed sentence using a noun a verb and another noun and then just take out one of the nouns. After doing this for a while you will find other ways that will suit your own personal style for implementing this technique.

Open Conditions: This is when you use a word to modify another such as an adjective a verb or an adverb but it is unclear as to what word you want to modify.

Example:

"Speaking to you as an intelligent person…"

In this statement it is unclear who specifically meets the conditions for being the intelligent person. Is the intelligent person you or is the intelligent person me (its both in this instance)? The subject is unspecified so the listener will use conformation bias to get the answer, while the unconscious mind picks up both meanings simultaneously.

Example 2:

"Those are some interesting thoughts and people..."

In this statement there are conditions that are unclear. We do not know whether the speaker is saying that just thoughts are interesting or that the people are interesting also.

Open Conditions are important when employing your Force Intuition it will guide the listener to outcomes for them selves and apply them to you.

Vital Techniques:

Yes Sets: (Conditioning Agreement) Yes Set is a type of repetition cycle where one will intentionally assert numerous statements of obvious truths where the sole intention is to get the subject to repeat the word yes inside their mind, or give some kind of mental confirmation to your statements and/or questions numerous times.

103

Example:

"You are now reading this sentence." "And your eyes are moving." "You could be intrigued." "And it is ok to be intrigued, now isn't it"

As you can see the yes set gets the listener into a mental state of agreement. This is a valuable and powerful tool when it comes to using The Force because agreement helps create a connection with the wholeness of The Force. Some people may have already been exposed to this power and did not know why it works or where the power comes from but they do know how well it works and employee it nonetheless.

Feints: A Feint is a statement constructed to engage the subject while also narrowing down the field of different possibilities for future statements

Feints are great ways of prying for information without the listener being consciously aware of it. This is because some Feints can be posed as a statement and can be perceived as a question depending on the subjective bias of the listener.

Example:

"You like wearing red?"

Notice in the example above one is saying "You like wearing red?" as opposed to

"Do you like wearing red?" This slight difference is all it takes for the listener's Conformation Bias to kick in. If the listener likes wearing red Subjective Validation will take it as a statement, however if the listener does not like to wear red they will take it as a question.

Feints also use Subjective Validation to a higher degree than many other types of Numonic grammar techniques. Feints can also employ Noncommittals whereas you are not committing to one assertion or another just engaging for a reaction or some information from the listener. These are called Noncomittal Feints.

> Example:
> "I actually may know more about your destiny than you think I do?"

In the statement above you will see we used the Noncommittal "may" this gives the person employing Force Intuition a back door to the assertion because the statement is not totally committed.

Subconscious Heuristics: Unifies Grouping into thought clusters like all or none, sweeping generalizations and irrational associations. B&W and generalizing speech are often an element of a Subconscious Heuristic.

The world is naturally chaotic and people have to make sense of things all the time while having only limited knowledge, resources and time. This action causes people to filter through their current experience by putting those thoughts into thought clusters. This can be useful when applying Force Sensory powers because the underlying understanding is that our environments in which we evolved and now live in have certain norms, and that decision making both evolved and the socialized utilize these situation based norms.

These thought clusters or Heuristics have neurological relations to one another and can be used much like Groundless Equations. Take for instance a Dog or a Car in general terms these two things are seemingly unrelated however subconsciously they are because or our minds inherent way of clustering thoughts. When talking to someone you can unconsciously plant the number four within the listeners mind when using these two words together because the element of four is a subconscious connecter of the two. How so you may be wondering. The fact of the matter is that both a Dog and a Car use the number four for locomotion, (four legs and four wheels.) and subconsciously we know this even though it is not a typical socialized connection between the basic elements of the two items

Tag Questions: This is an old technique use by sales people and has probably been around longer than recorded history. Is the act of adding a subtle question of positive assurance after one makes a statement. One will often make use of a tag question to invite the listener to concur with ones certainty about the specific subject matter, or to just guide their mind subconsciously.

Example:

"Learning this will make you stronger... won't it?" or "You like learning about The Force... don't you?"

Tag questions are great to use with Yes sets and are very effective when one uses them as an inflection to ones commands and/ or statements.

Synchronizing: Describe what someone is doing or what experiences are happening at the moment that happen to be obviously true. This kind of pacing is similar to a yes set but they always have something to do with what is going on with the listener at that moment. (As you sit there you may notice the feeling of the pages on your fingers.) This technique is great when using Force Persuasion and provides you with the ability to easily guide the thought process of the listener. Its impact is even more effective if you have the listener take notice of things they probably aren't focusing consciously on. Have them follow your synchronization for a bit and then start mentally leading them into another direction of your bidding instead of just arbitrarily following their obvious sensory stimulation.

This technique works best when you fluctuate between both Synchronizing and

107

leading. (Synchronize- Synchronize- Synchronize- Lead- Synchronize- Lead-Synchronize- Synchronize-Lead- Lead)

This is one of the techniques where you can feel The Force Power flow through you the most. There will be a connection that will occur between you and whoever you are using it on. It will enlighten both of you even more to your connection with The Force, because you will feel it blatantly surge inside of you with this technique. I believe this is because of the intimate connection created while using this technique.

Inferring Choice: Most people like to have the feeling that they are making a choice about something however the allusion of having that choice in the first place is what takes the listener off guard.

When you are Inferring Choice in the listener you have to control the context of what is being said. Controlling the context controls the listener's point of reference. If you can control the point of reference you control the listeners perception and with that their idea of choice. Take for instance a parent that says to their children that they have to go to bed early if they don't eat their peas, compared to a parent that says that if you eat your peas you can stay up later. Controlling the context of what the bed time is and the eating of the peas creates an Inferred Choice in the listening child. Yet both are trying to accomplish the same end result.

Another technique you should learn is that the act of making two or more requests from someone is also a method of creating the illusion of choice.

Making two requests of the listener is an excellent way of covering your bases. The reason it works is because most people will consciously focus on answering the question according to a list of requirements.

Example: "Would you like to go to the seminar this Summer or Fall?"

Most people with this question will put the majority of their conscious concentration on answering when they will go to the Seminar. While doing this the true focus of the statement, going to the Seminar, is usually overlooked, and becomes a hidden command.

Take note, that when using this technique, that there is always an implied outcome that typically goes unnoticed. The question is simply left to the receiver of the message as to how and when the message will be carried out.

Command Mask: Is a command formed as a question to give the illusion of conscious control to the listener.

Example:

"Can you take a look at your hands for a moment?"

This is a one of the most primary techniques when using Force Persuasion because it is such a passive way to give a command to someone. This is best done with tonal accents as well.

When using the technique you will want to inflect your vocal tone.

Reality Breach: This is the act of one giving conscious attributes to something or someone that does not necessarily have those attributes.

Example:

"This book is wise." or "The walls can hear what you are saying?"

Your subject will subconsciously assign such attributes to you. This technique may also be employed when wishing to misdirect the attribute to ones subject instead.

Example:

"That is amazing how you did that!" or "Your mind is connecting to mine."

110

During these times the subject will make a personal connection to such radical statements and connect the statements to them selves. In both cases, the subject will subconsciously decide how to make these statements fit within their own personal experience using a combination of conformation bias and subjective validation.

Chronological Tuning (Chronos Studies): The control of participles to place and/or change time related events in the mind of the listener.

The tenses of verbs, for example, can subconsciously shape the listeners innate sense of time. As in past tense, present tense and future tense. These tenses can place a thought in a specific area of time with in the mind of the listener.

Remember that it is not only the words that you speak that give you the power; it is the intent with which you use them. The nature of your desires is what makes The Force powerful. If your heart is corrupt, then your results will be far less than extraordinary, but If your heart is just then you will become more powerful than you could ever imagine.

Section 5:

Numinetics -The use of Body Language with Subconscious Communication

Have you ever wondered how certain beings who wielded The Force could read the minds of others, how they could prophesize and impending future? It is believed that through The Force one may witness the thoughts and feelings of others and Numinetics is the path to how it is done. The reason these Masters of The Force could do these things is because they developed the ability of Force Intuition through Numinetics and this in turn helps channel The Force though them to help guide them.

Numinetics is a skill that enables you to understand an unspoken language from just about anybody you ever have come in contact with. Numinetics is one of the most extensive and valuable Force abilities. It can be utilized to see another being's feelings, to peer into the future or sometimes even predict impending danger. It is a telepathic like intuition endowed to us by the power of The Force.

Have you ever met someone, such as a friend's friend or a new coworker, and got a strange negative feeling that overwhelmed you when you met them? Inside you knew that there was just something amiss about that person, something that you didn't quite trust. Maybe a gut feeling that the person had done something horribly wrong or maybe they just weren't very trustworthy in your eyes. In the end you found out you had been right about them all along. This is The Force working through you.

Have you ever had an intuition that foresaw something that a friend, or even a stranger, was going to do before they did it? Have you ever had the feeling that you just knew something somebody was going to say before they even uttered a single word? That quirky feeling inside can be a bit confusing and can perhaps be even a little eerie at times. It might have even made you feel as if you had some kind of telepathic powers. I am going to tell you that that weird little feeling is quite normal and it is only The Force speaking to you. The Force allows you to witness the thoughts and feelings of other people and things. In this next section we are going to develop that part of The Force within you and then amplify it so you can use it more effectively.

Numinetics is one of the most fundamental of all Force abilities. It can be used to feel another being's feelings, their thoughts and sometimes the future. Numinetics is a Force power deeply connected with Force Senses, and involves picking up impressions of an individual's emotional state by paying attention to their nonverbal cues and micro-movements. It is a telepathic like intuition endowed to us by the power of The Force. Let me explain to you how. Mind reading is a term used in psychology to simply explain the subconscious observation and study of nonverbal cues, such as conscious and/or subconscious body movements and facial expressions. Some people have unconsciously learned how to use these movements to determine the emotional states of others. This is the same reason as to why you felt those feelings about that person we were talking about earlier.

Mind reading is a latent ability that many of us have and something that many people do all the time, but it is not intentionally controlled. The fact of the matter is that people tend to only do it subconsciously. With out the power of The Force and the knowledge of Numinetics this ability would be left to only to the subconscious mind, however we do have the advantage of having these things. We have the ability to tap into that part of our subconscious and consciously condition our instincts to be able to do it at will. However we must train our minds to recognize such things so we can control it. The control is a mental ability and it is ones duty to discipline ones self with this knowledge so it can grant the unforeseen knowledge of The Force. Numinetics is a skill that will teach you how to control these interactions and will enable you to observe and differentiate the thoughts and feelings inside other people.

In this section of the book we are going be enlightened on how to consciously condition our brains so that we can apply these typically subconscious abilities to a conscious advantage. This will give us the ability to utilize these skills so we may more accurately predict the internal states and external actions of others by a simple conscious evaluation of their mannerisms and nonverbal cues.

The Numinetic Probe:

This is the ability to observe others subconscious body activity such as minute movements of the facial muscles, shifts of the eyes, the changing of skin color, adjustments in breathing rate and rhythm, or certain tilts of the head. These movements can usually be associated to certain thought processes and emotions. Most movements telegraph intent and in doing so they help us to read the specific thought patterns of the person we are interacting with. For instance, people will often look upwards as they visualize an image in their mind, or flare their nostrils as they recall a specific smell. The Force resides in a person's mind and feelings, knowing the Numinetic Probe will allow you to recognize those thoughts and feelings by simple observation.

Did you know that there are cell structures in the brain that focus on distinguishing familiar patterns in the world around us? Defining things like certain spectrums of color, the feelings of a specific textures or even particular frequencies of sound. Within these cell structures are even more complicated combinations of cells that are geared towards exceptionally more complex tasks such as distinguishing facial features, head movements and even body language. There are even groups of neurons that are geared to predict and plan body movements.

After learning these types of movements you will become much more familiar with them and in doing so you will garner the ability of the Numinetic Probe to read people with a high level of effectiveness. This will help you with your endeavors at channeling The Force and employing Force Intuition. SO let us begin learning about the various Numinetic Probes.

Head Gesticulation:

Head Gesticulation is the heads ability to covey messages. Head gestures have the have always had the ability to telegraph a wide range of information and they differ from that of just the face or other parts that are above the shoulders. Because of this in the following chapter we will primarily focus on the movement of the head as affected by the neck muscles. The face and other parts of the head will be covered in later sections dedicated solely to those subject matters.

Lowering of the Head: Lowering of the head is when the chin is use to cover the neck. This is an unconscious defense posture of the chin protecting the neck from a perceived danger. In more primitive times the perceived danger was most often quite real, however in modern times the threat of physical harm to the vulnerable neck is quite

116

minuscule. Typically the defensive mechanism sets in now as a result from when one feels emotionally or verbally threatened.

When one lowers their head sometimes the eyes will lower also to avert ones gaze. Based on primitive instincts a weaker or lesser member of a group staring into the eyes of an alpha or higher member may be construed as a threat or an act of aggression against that member. The act of lowering ones head and avoiding eye contact minimizes any confusion with in the pecking order. Therefore the act of averting ones eyes while lowering ones head is usually accepted as a sign of submission

Sometimes we lower our head with a brief quick movement know as a nod. The nod is commonly accepted as a confirmation or an agreement of some kind. This is important because when you are in a conversation and you notice the unconscious head nod it signals you that what you are saying is being accepted by the listener. Usually the intensity of the not will correlate with the intensity of the agreement. So if they are nodding fast they are in more agreement if they are nodding slowly they probably are a little more skeptical about the assertion. Sometimes the nod originates out of arrogance though. A granting that the listener will consider what you have to say at least to some extent.

Last but not least a head nod in the Far East is generally accepted as a greeting and sign of respect. Even though I have not read any study to say other wise I believe

117

this also goes back to our primitive ancestral sign of submission.

Raising of the Head: Many times when you see someone raise their head it is because something has peaked their interest. Again coming from primitive times a lift of the head would help you see if there was danger or prey somewhere with in the vicinity. Also when there is a sound of interest or one that is of low volume most people tend to perk up an ear causing the head to raise, again a sign of interest. This form of head raising is usually accompanied with a slight eyebrow raise or widening of the pupils (which is discussed more in the Pupillometrics section of the book). When done quickly the movement tends to be a sign of inquiry. A kind of asking such as "What were you saying?"

The raising of the head can also mean the exact opposite as well. It can be the act of boredom however this is usually accompanied with a roll of the eyes or the act of looking up towards the eyebrows instead of the other eye cues associated with interest. At this time the person most likely is making pictures in their head and not listening to you (this is covered more in the Optic Movement Analysis OMA part of the book).

Left Right Movements: Have you ever seen some one say no? If you had you have seen the infamous shaking of the head that came with it. This turning of the head form side to side as you well know is a sign of disagreement. Some theorist believe that this movement originated from the socialized conditioning from when we were infants

118

and was a way of moving our heads out of the way to refuse food or other items to be placed in our mouths. This turning of the head has translated into our everyday body language as in when someone turns their head away in disapproval or in avoidance of communication for the moment. Note that some people will not do these movements so obviously and only do it slightly as a form of pretext or self control.

At times the turn of the head may just be because of physiology and the inability to hear the other person that is speaking. It could also be something as simple as inattentiveness because something else has peaked their interest. When something peaks someone's interest their faces will usually point in the direction of what ever had peaked that interest turning the head either left or right. Again look for micromovements for people trying to disguise their intentions.

Visage

(The Art of Reading the Face):

Skill does not have to draw primarily from The Force, ones sensitivity and conditioning can allow one to understand as well. As you are reading this paragraph you may want to take notice of the words and punctuations that have actually created it. What really makes up these sentences and the underlying meanings that are attributed to them? In reality you what are looking at are series of abstract lines and shapes that we have associated certain ideas to and when we combine it we call it language. Why do we do this? We do this so we may communicate more effectively with one another, so basically it's a system to communicate better. This is the skill of language and Numinetics enables one to understand the unspoken language of the mind of any sentient being they are interacting with. The art of Visage will grant you the ability to witness the thoughts and feelings of others, although it does not necessarily allow one to relate to that person, it will allow you to know their thought patterns.

As noted earlier ideas can be communicated through the act of reading the written word. Words are made up of letters, twenty six to be exact if you are a using the Roman alphabet and words are put together into sentences by using punctuation. All together they create a language. What if I told you that you were able to read the mind of a person just like you are reading this book? Well you can. Just like words have the letters of the alphabet the face has its own alphabet and also its own punctuations too. The face is an amazing instrument of communication and facial expressions are an inherent part of our nature as human beings.

Paul Ekman's Facial Action Coding System (F.A.C.S.): In 1978 two highly accomplished scientists by the name of Ekman and Friesen had created a system for systematically measuring and analyzing people's facial expressions and movements.

The system that they created was called F.A.C.S. or Facial Action Coding System.

This system was put together by studying the particular musculature anatomy of the face and the explicit movements that are associated with it. By developing F.A.C.S. Ekman and Friesten were able to connect these specific facial arrangements to the emotions that related to them.

Since then F.A.C.S. became a very successful tool utilized in various fields for recognizing and interpreting facial expressions. It has been used for movies and videogames to make the characters look more real to life, it has been used by anthropologist for forensic reconstruction of ancient faces, but more importantly it is now being used for counter intelligence for national security. Federal counter intelligence agencies have been using F.A.C.S. because it breaks down facial expressions into basic pieces called Action Units. Ekman is always adding to his list of action units but we for now are only going to use only forty six of them. National security agencies are programming computers to recognize these units so they may learn to read peoples faces and also their intentions. Connecting these computers to security cameras they predict that they will be able to catch would be terrorists by the analyzing of there microexpressions and curtail any future wrong doing. Action Units are not restricted to being just the muscles in the face but more so the actions that the facial muscles can perform. There are more than ten thousand possible facial expressions that have been measured so far. This in turn gives you over ten thousand ways of reading into someone's internal emotional state. Here is the list of the Action Units you can look at them as if they were like the twenty six letters in the alphabet.

1.   Inner Brow Raiser   (Frontalis, Pars Medialis)

AU01
Inner Brow Raiser

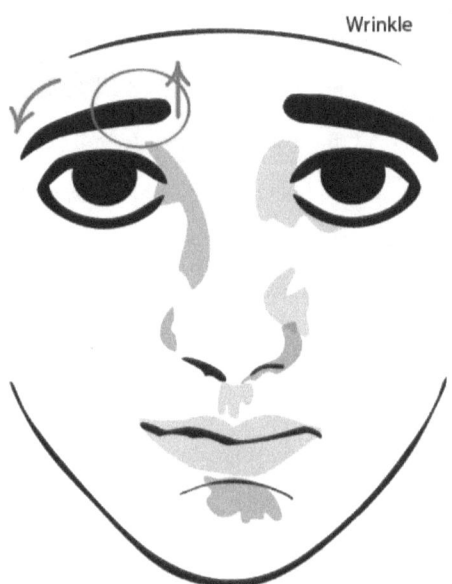

2.   Outer Brow Raiser   (Frontalis, Pars Lateralis)

AU02

Wrinkle

3. *There is no #03AU*

4. Brow Lowerer   (Depressor Glabellae, Depressor Supercilli;

Corrugator)

AU04
Brow Lowerer

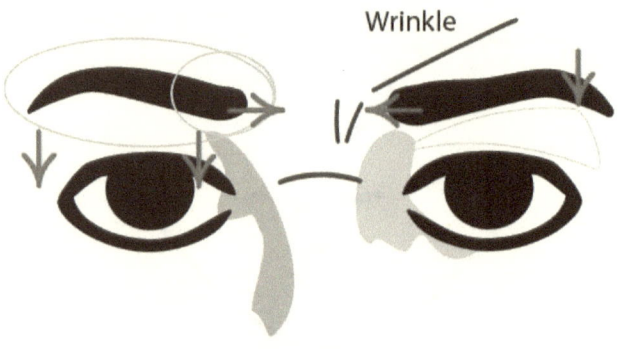

5.   Upper Lid Raiser   (Levator Palpebrae Superioris)

AU05
Upper Lid Raiser

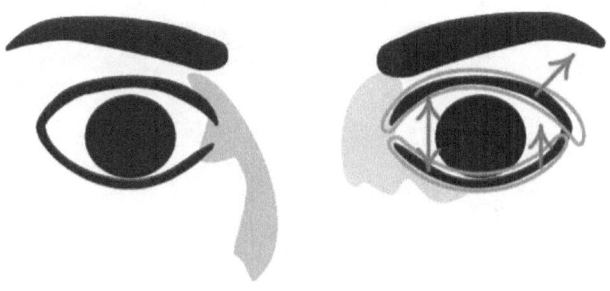

6.   Cheek Raiser   (Orbicularis Oculi, Pars Orbitalis) *No graphic available*

7.   Lid Tightener   (Orbicularis Oculi, Pars Palebralis)

AU07
Lid Tightener

8.   *There is not #AU08*

9.   Nose Wrinkler   (Levator Labii Superioris, Alaeque Nasi)

AU09
Nose Wrinkler

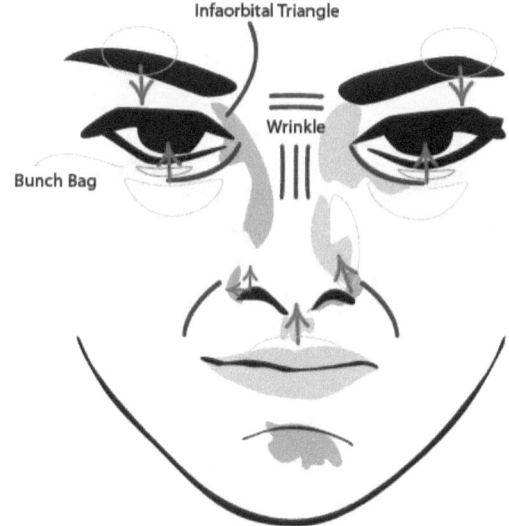

10. Upper Lip Raiser   (Levator Labii Superioris, Caput

Infraorbitalis)

AU010
Upper Lip Raise

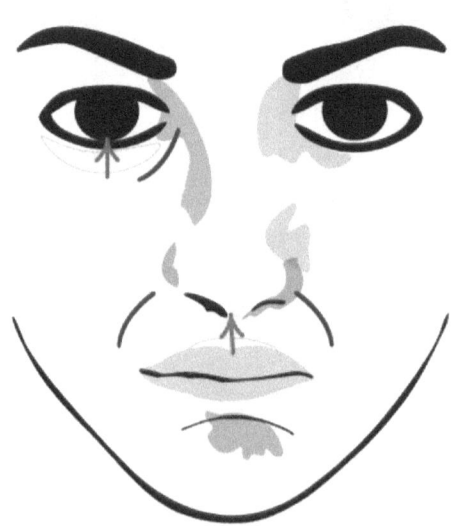

11.   Nasolabial Fold Deepener   (Zygomatic Minor)

AU11
Nasolabial Furrow Deepener

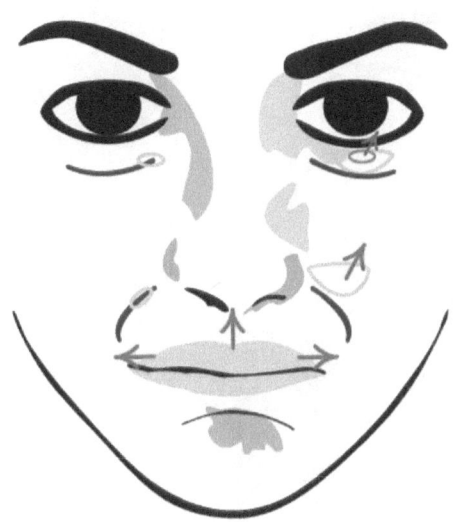

12. Lip Corner Puller   (Zygomatic Major)

AU12
Lip Corner Puller

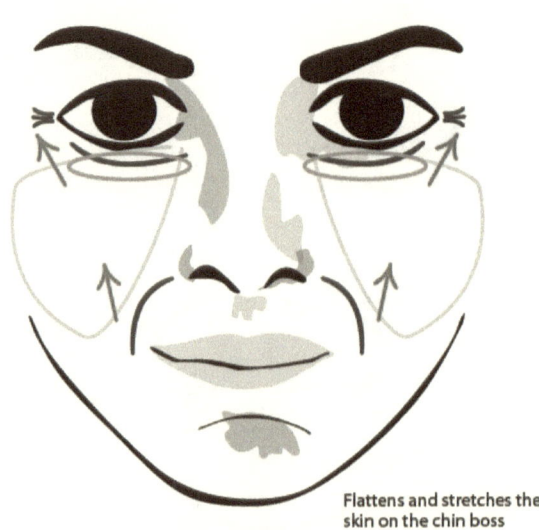

Flattens and stretches the
skin on the chin boss

13.   Cheek Puffer   (Caninus)

AU13
Sharp Lip Puller

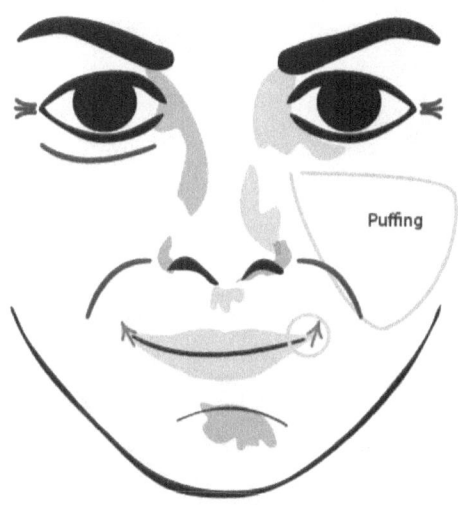

Puffing

14. Dimpler (Buccinator)

132

15.   Lip Corner Depressor   (Triangularis)

AU15
Lip Corner Depressor

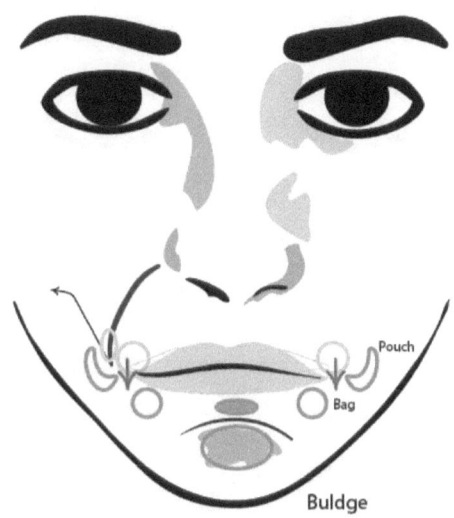

16.   Lower Lip Depressor   (Depressor Labii)

AU16
Lower Lip Depressor

17.　　Chin Raiser　(Mentalis)

AU17
Chin Raiser

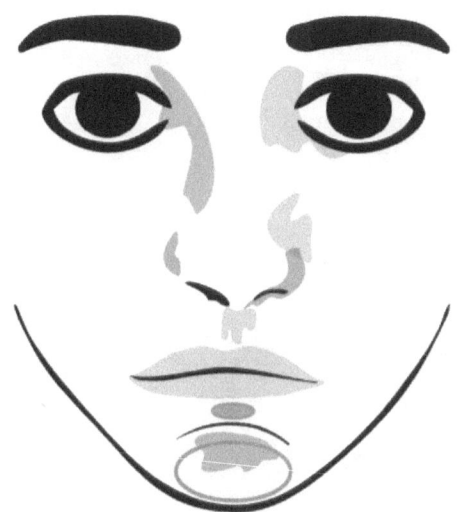

18. Lip Puckerer   (Incisivii Labii Superioris; Incisivii Labii Inferioris)

AU18
Lip Pucker

19. Tongue out   *No graphic available*

136

20. Lip Stretcher (Risorius)

AU20
Lip Stretcher

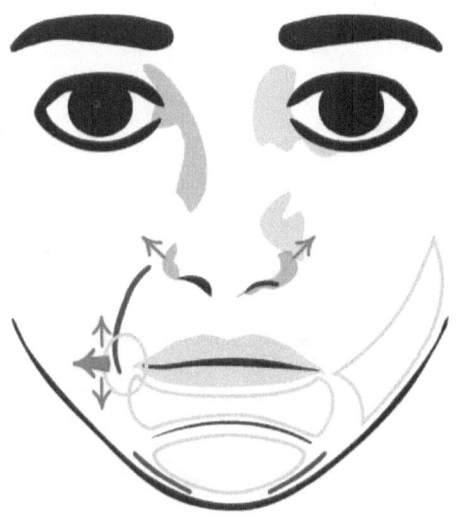

21. Neck Tightener   *No graphic available*

22. LipFunneler (Orbicularis Oris)   *No graphic available*

23. Lip Tightener (Orbicularis Oris)   *No graphic available*

24.   Lip Pressor   (Orbicularis Oris)

AU24
Lip Presser

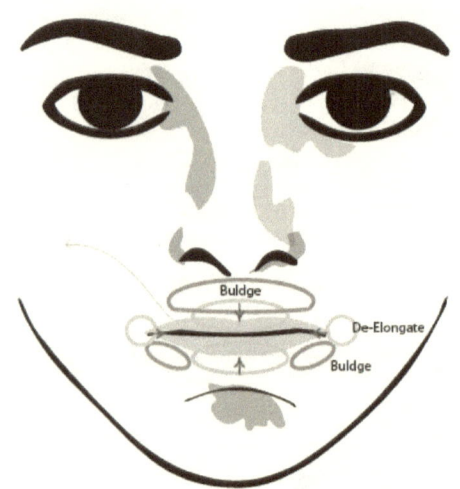

25.   Lips Part   (Depressor Labii, or Relaxation of Mentalis or

Orbicularis Oris)

Au25
Lips Part

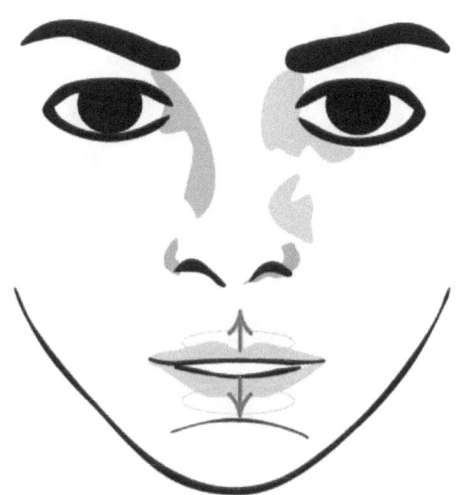

26.   Jaw Drop   (Masetter; Temporal and Internal Pterygoid

Relaxed)

Au26
Jaw Drop

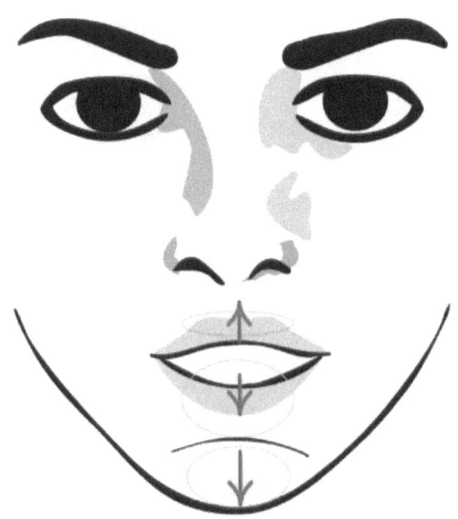

27. Mouth Stretch   (Pterygoids; Digastric)

Au27
Mouth Stretch

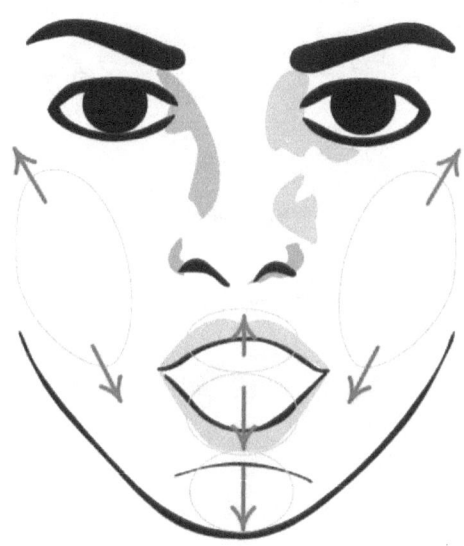

28.   Lip Suck   (Orbicularis Oris)

AD28
Lip Suck

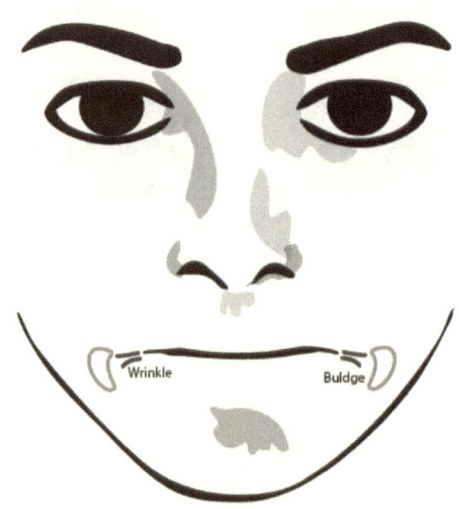

142

29.   Jaw Thrust

AD29
Jaw Thrust

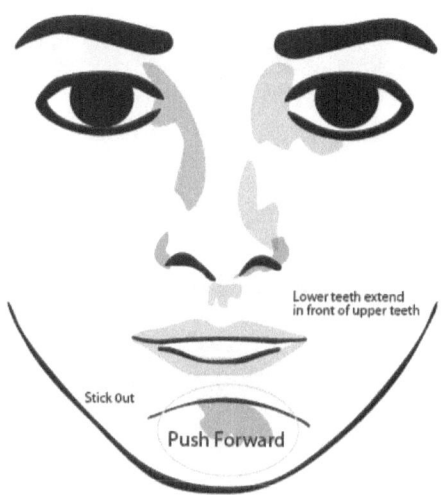

Lower teeth extend
in front of upper teeth

Stick Out

Push Forward

30.   Jaw Sideways

AU30
Jaw Sideways

31.   Jaw Clencher   *No graphic avilable*

144

32. Lip Bite   *No graphic available*

33. Cheek Blow

AD33
Blow

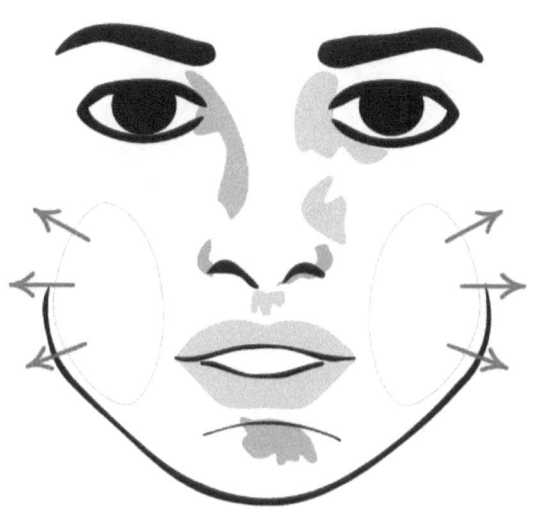

34. Cheek Puff *No graphic available*

35. Cheek Suck *No graphic available*

36.   Tongue Bulge

AU36
Buldge

37.   Lip Wipe   *No graphic available*

38.   Nostril Dilator   *No graphic available*

39.   Nostril Compressor

AU39
Nostril Compressor

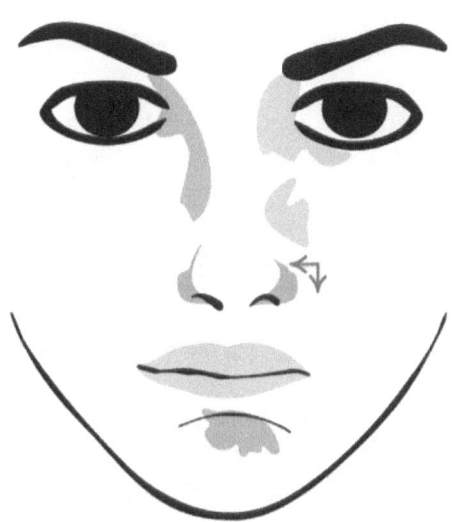

41.   Lid Droop

AU41
Lid Drop

42.   Slit

AU42
Slit

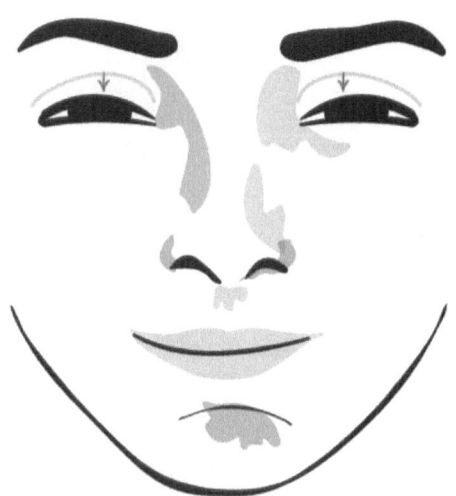

43.   Eyes Closed

AU43
Eyes Closed

150

44.   Squint

AU44
Squint

45.   Blink

AU45
Blink

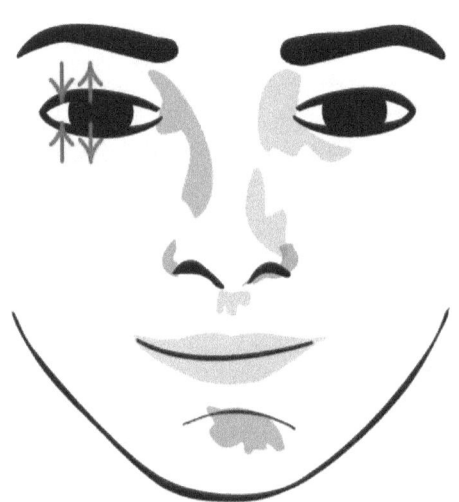

46. Wink

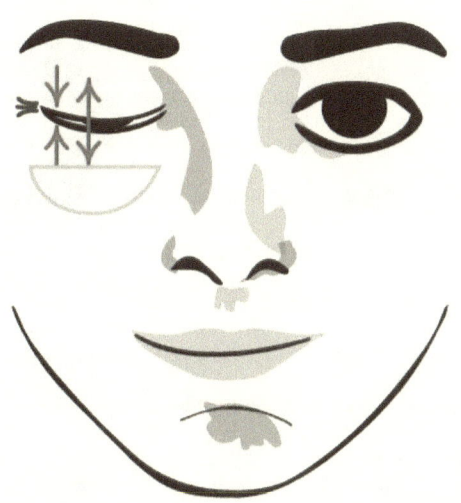

153

Put together these Action Units and they will give you all the tools needed to be able to read the intentions in another's face through their microexpressions. By understanding these AU's and conditioning yourself to notice them you will be able to read anyone's emotional state or true feelings by just a simple glance. Each AU combines with others to indicate specific internal states. Just like specific letters arranged together create specific words. There is a whole dictionary to be learned so it is like learning a entirely new language. Here is an exercise to get you started so you can become better at noticing them.

Exercise (1): This activity is going to need at least two people so it can be done properly. First write down on some index cards a series specific internal states. You can write obvious ones like Fear, Anger, Happiness, and Love. You should also get creative and write down some of the not so obvious states too like Anxiety, Confidence, Openness, and Accepting. I am sure you can think of others there is a plethora to choose from. On a separate piece of paper you want to make a list of those same internal states that you wrote on the cards. Deal the cards to each person face down and they are not to show them to anyone else. At this point in the game whoever is first must get into the state mentioned in the card. Have them think about an occurrence that put them in that state in the past. While in state the others will take turns trying to guess what state it is. Whoever gets it right gets to be the one to get in state next. After being correctly predicted you need to write down the Action Units that were noticed on the paper with the list. After playing the game a few times you will begin to notice certain patterns, some common to everyone and some unique to specific people. You will also notice that certain Action Units will come up again and again for certain states remembering these action units will help you when it comes to reading strangers and also when you want to educate others on how to read peoples internal states.

Ones emotional expression can play a critical role in our day to day interactions with others. Often, these emotions are displayed to others and signal important nonverbal cues to another's emotional states. Our face to face expressions adjust according to our interactions with different personalities in different situations. As shown earlier these expressions can be read and interpreted to mean that the sender a specific emotions or thinking a certain thought but you must learn how to gauge it.

Eye Cues:

(This does not work on Schizophrenics) One has been typically socialized to think of the eye only as an information receiver; however when using The Force one must assume that the eyes also plays the role of an information transmitter. One may have the ability to consciously manipulate and control verbal language; however the eyes have numerous amounts of unintentional shifts attributed to them. These latent and subtle eye movements reveal the true meaning behind someone else's thoughts and/or intentions.

These movements can be so specific it's as if they have a private language unto themselves and because of this the eyes truly are the windows to the soul.

"We carry our eye values into our feelings about other species."

Desmond Morris: Man Watching 1977

The eye's role as an information transmitter comes from its function as a signal receiver and therefore it is spontaneous. If you want to gather information about someone you have to direct your eyes towards the person you want to gather data on. This action creates some vulnerability between the two of you. However you now have the ability to read the other person and the subject may also be able to read just as easily into you as well.

"Breaking off social communication by averting the gaze is recognized as
avoidance, unlikely to be followed by action."

Eckhard Hess: The Tell Tail Eye 1975

Everyday our lives show us numerous examples that how important eye signals are in our day to day interactions, and how difficult they are to manipulate voluntarily. Many social interactions are now becoming digital and we lose many of these valuable intricacies in communication because of it. This is leading people further away from The Force by creating a disassociation between one another which in turn weakens The Force.

Pupillometrics: There is an art to reading peoples eyes some do it naturally and with relative ease in the same way that Mozart could write a symphony while others may need to work at it and learn what chords, octaves and measures are. There are movements with in the eye that could be related to chords, octaves and measures and some of these movements are called Pupillometrics. These are movements within the pupil that act as a supportive mechanism to the Autonomic Nervous System. In turn the Autonomic Nervous System will send signals that activate variations in the pupil's size in accordance to particular emotional stimulation. To become astute at reading another's inside dialog it is in your best interest to become consciously aware of which emotional states trigger these visible changes. Knowledge of which emotional states fire these specific changes will give you an extraordinary amount of insight into the subject's internal condition. In other words watching the subject's pupils will give you even more access to their minds. The how and what they are thinking which in turn increases your Force Intuition abilities.

Dilation- Arousal (positive and negative), Interest, Increased Effort Mental and Physical, Mental Processing Space (Eyes will reach maximum Dilation when max mental space is used), Anticipation, Submissiveness, Attentive, Appeasing mood and Sympathy

Contraction- Unpleasant Stimulus, Disinterest, Mental Capacity Overload,

Ocular Movement Analysis (OMA): Pupillometrics are just one of the ways that the eyes communicate. Another way that our eyes communicate is by the movements in which they make. The direction that the eyes move and the patterns that follow telegraph volumes about what is going on inside ones subject.

When people are thinking and talking they have a tendency to shift their eyes around. These movements are a common byproduct form the reflection and processing of the information being shared.

159

The belief is that when a person creates a new thought upon a topic, or reflects upon the data being shared, that person will move their eyes around to give ocular cues of how they are thinking. These movements are considered by some to be an indication of the internal representation the subject is using during the time they are evaluating the subject matter.

Many performing Mentalists and Magicians trust this theory and use eye cues as an indicator to what kind of thought patterns are happening within the person they are working with. The way they do this is by asking questions and looking where the eyes move to get their cue. Using visual cues of internal thought progressions is quite an easy task however it takes a little conditioning to get you to do it regularly.

The First thing you want to do is think of the eye as a clock meaning looking up would be twelve o'clock and looking down would be six o'clock. Using the clock model as an indicator helps gauge the way the mind accesses thought. The second thing you want do is ask questions to the person you want to gauge the eye cue form, something like where they lived when they were a child. After asking the question the person will move their eyes in a certain direction. Then mentally notate the movement and then ask a similar question, such as what kind of bike they had, to calibrate if that eye cue is accurate or not. If the eyes move in the same direction you have a good eye cue indicator for remembering. Now ask them to imagine something they would of liked to of had but did not as a child, a toy or something, and have imagine they had it and were playing with it. Look where their eye moves and take a mental note. Then ask them to think about their mother being shorter or taller than she was. Watch their eyes again if it goes to the same place you have a good calibration of where their eyes go when the subject is imagining something.

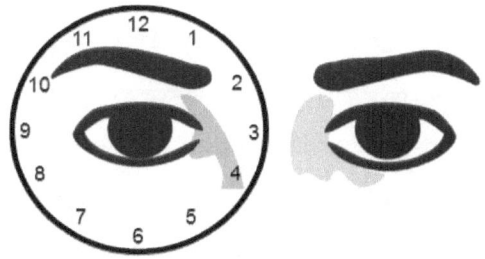

Many police officers and detectives are taught these indicators to see when someone is lying however they are given universal eye cues that have been shown in several studies to be unreliable. The OMA technique taught here may take more practice however it is much more accurate because you must gauge eye cues to each person as an individual then make your assessments from there.

The Breath:

The act of being conscious of another's breath is a skill not customarily taught to people. It is in fact an insight that only few know. Many accomplished Masters of The Force would condition their sight to notice such movements and were able to amplify their Force Persuasion and Force Intuition powers because of it. In this section of the book we will be going over the breath and the implications of different types of breathing. The way we breathe has a direct impact on our biochemistry and thus our neurology. This is because it regulates the oxygen intake of our bodies and the chemical composition of our blood. Breathing from different areas and the variable rates can have a profound impact on the brains internal workings and our emotional states. There fore it can be a powerful indicator of the internal state.

It should be said being mindful of breathing in and of itself isn't going to help you read other people that much, although the combination of this technique with other Numinetic Projections will give you the insights you desire.

Heavy Breathing: It is pretty common for people to breath through the two orifices in the middle of their face called the nostrils, but every now and then the body

162

will need a bit more oxygen and its way of getting it is through the mouth.

Sometimes a person will become upset, worried or angry during a conversation. When these emotions start to occur the fight or flight mechanism is unconsciously initiated and breathing will become heavier. This is because in primitive times more oxygen was needed in preparation for oncoming combat that may ensue because of the situation or the fleeing one might have to do if one were unable to protect oneself. More blood was needed for the muscles in those situations so heavier breathing ensued. Some people experiencing these emotions may try to subdue them and will allow their mouth to hang open to get more oxygen.

Be watchful of their stomach or chest. These are great gauges of how deeply the person is breathing. If the person is breathing from their chest it is a good sign that there mood is more extroverted during this time. Where as one who is breathing from the stomach is typically a sign of a more introverted state. A little more covert way to observe someone's breathing patterns is to pay attention to their shoulders. The speed in which you notice the rise and fall of shoulders will indication where they are breathing from. A more rapid movement is an indicator of chest breathing where as a slower movements usually indicates stomach breathing.

Deep Inhalations: Slow, deep breathing is often associated with someone who is in a relaxed state. Slow breathing can also be an indication of some sort of disinterest, boredom as you may. Many times deep breathing will occur in the stomach because of the latent connection between being relaxed or disinterested and introspectiveness. Use your peripheral vision and take heed of how the stomach expands and the rate in which it does so.

Short deep breathing, specifically when they are in succession or in a type of rhythm, are typically veiled sobs and consequently an indicator of suppressing some sort of trauma or sadness

Numinetic Projection:

Skin color is typically subject to the amount of melanin in the skin itself. Most of the skin variations we see from day to day are due to genetic and environmental reasons. However in this section we are going to pay more attention on how the flow of blood effects color changes within ones face.

When looking at the face you may want to pay close attention to the variations in the skins tonus. When I say skin tonus I am referring to the color or under color of the skin. Although there are many different people with many different skin colors we are only going to pay attention to the underlying hues of the skin and there are two primary ones that will be our main focus. The first is the reddening of the skin and the second is when the skin becomes pale.

Reddening: Red is usually a color that denotes an arousal of the sympathetic nerve, which oversees the fight or flight instinct in human beings. It is why our blood vessels contract, why our palms sweat, why our heart beats faster, but most importantly, for this area of focus, it is why we blush. Red often times is a color that denotes a change in ones blood flow or extra blood being consumed within a person. We know that when a person is hot, the blood will come to the surface of the skin to cool itself down, manifesting itself as a nice rosy glow in the person's appearance

There are generally two ways that blood temperature typically raises, one of the ways is from the act of physical exertion. When someone lifts weights or is trying to move something that doesn't seem to budge their face usually becomes red this is because of human thermodynamics. The next way and the one we are going to focus on is the one equated to emotional arousal.

The appearance of red in the face can be associated to several internal emotional states such as a person who is either irritated or a person who is angry. Anger and irritation are two emotions that produce some of the strongest reactions within the sympathetic nerve.

Anxiety in many cases will also lead to redness in the face especially if the person is extremely shy or are feeling stress from social anxiety disorder. A strong red tone can also be an indicator of shame and/or embarrassment. Many times when a person has done something wrong, made a mistake, or were in a shameful situations their reaction often times will include an act of blushing.

Out of all the acts of blushing I feel that embarrassment is the most commonly known it too signifies emotional arousal by portraying a rosy glow. There are many people who seem to blatantly blush when they are embarrassed and there are some that are more subtle yet they still blush nonetheless.

There are certain signs of facial reddening are pretty obvious to most people, signs like when someone's cheeks turn red, yet with others it maybe their entire face that turns red however there are people out there that only their neck will turn red. They are not as easily noticed however this will give you an added insight so that you may notice them in the future.

When the skin becomes pale: In general the face will pale when blood drains from it and there are a few reasons for this phenomenon to happen. The first is becoming stunned (I refer to the word stunned instead of shocked because I do not want any misunderstanding from the medical definition of shock); pale cheeks are a typical sign when a person becomes startled or surprised by something they are not ready for. Paling skin is also an indication of extreme fear which slightly differs from just being startled because ones well being is at stake. Have you ever heard to the expression "pale as a ghost?" Well that is because when someone is frightened the blood is moved from places like the skin to the muscles where it is more readily needed. The purpose is to better enable the ability to flee or react to what ever produced the initial fear

A person who becomes pale can also be a sign of someone who is emotionally stressed as well as physical stressed. Paling skin may be a sign of someone being cold because the blood goes deep so it may move more regular and to avoid cooling from the external elements. Someone's white skin may also be because of a lack of sun exposure. Pale skin can also be a sign that someone is anemic and is deficient in Iron, Folic Acid or Vitamin B12. It can be a result from shock or even an upset stomach

As you can see Numinetics is one of the most insightful Force abilities. It can be used to peer into the thoughts of others without relying on their words, connect to another being's feelings and even predict the ever uncertain future. The future predictions take shape from ones own conditioned instincts by calibrating the finer points of the subjects emotionally associated movements, and then predicting the probable outcome for the next course of action. Numinetics teaches you to train your sight to notice certain movements and in doing so it amplifies your ability to perform Force Persuasion and Force Intuition because of it. As you can see there is no magic behind what we do. The power of The Force is merely drawn from the living beings around us, because it is what connects all living beings.

167

Chapter 5: Secret of the Seers:

Putting it all Together

Throughout this book we have been examining the enigmatic power of The Force. We have learned some the intricate facets of why it works and some of the essential tools to evoke its awesome power. During this chapter we are going to discover how to apply some of these mysterious methods of The Force Sensory powers that you've learned about in the previous chapters. We will do this by showing how one can combine the various elements of Numinations to create a unique and amazing rapport building mind trick. We will also be focusing on how to channel the power of Force Intuition for everyday use in a much more of a detailed fashion in this section as well. These acts will help you cultivate what you have learned and give you experience you need so you can develop some custom mind tricks for yourself or with others if you wish to do so.

In this section I am going to explain a tactic that employees the action of Force Intuition. It is an approach that combines the nuances of both Force Intuition and Numinetic structuring. It is a technique that is great for establishing a mystical shroud of mystique about you, while creating a deep connection with the recipient. However, before we go any further let me ask you a question. Have you ever met someone new who seemed to know more about you than even some of your closest friends? Someone who unwittingly knew intimate details about some of the experiences you have gone through or some of the things you may have done. Someone who even knew surprisingly some of your deep dark secrets or maybe they foretold an event that was to come to be within your own future? Can you imagine what it would be like if you knew the secret behind this Mind Trick?

To have a Mind Trick in your arsenal so remarkable that it appeared to others that you had the amazing ability of a clairvoyant or even a telepath, a technique that creates the illusion that you could peer into someone's mind. Just imagine having this power as a tool and avoiding getting out of a speeding ticket, or even persuading ones way into just about anything.

Well I am going to teach you how to develop and cultivate this amazing power in The Force in order for you to build a higher connection with The Force. The specific use

169

of Force Sensory mind trick that you will be learning is called "Secret of the Seers". It is a technique that focuses on The Force Sensory powers and utilizing the Numonic Lexicon that you had gone over earlier in this book.

In this chapter we will also give you an outline on the Numinetic structure so you can follow along and perform the Secret yourself. "Secret of the Seers" will teach you how to habituate your conversations so that you will be able to be perceived by others as having a supernatural ability to read minds. Remember it is best to use the technique with someone; that you do not know them very well, and or someone that you not already have already established any amount of rapport prior. Please remember this is just one of the ways that you can use the building blocks of Numinations (the method for cultivating Force sensory powers) to use The Force, there are many others. It is just a great example on how to put the methodology of Numinations together so you can create Force Sensory techniques on your own.

The "Secret of the Seers" is based on a combination of various techniques that mystics, psychics, and fortune tellers have been using for centuries - the same techniques that neighborhood psychics use to have seemingly mysterious and supernatural powers. These assorted techniques are quite easy to master and their effects are long lasting and indeed mesmerizing.

Now for one to come to understand the "Secret of the Seers" one must become familiar with a few significant and fundamental principles of The Force. These simple rules you are now about to discover are very important for achieving the impression of your empathic power while creating that special kind of connection with someone. These rules are specifically important for when one has little or no prior information about the certain person that one is going to use Force Intuition on. Before we get started I must state that it is essential to memorize and master the rules of Numinations that were laid down in the earlier sections. They will be crucial to the implementation of The Force as they allow you to employ Force Powers with minimal to no effort. Examine the techniques over and over again until you have a thorough understanding of how to use them and how the outcome is achieved. Dedication to your ultimate potential is made by accepting the fact that you must practice. For it is through the fundamentals of Numinations that you will be able to impose your new found supernatural influence upon others.

Section 1:

A Sequence of Actions

The first thing we want to do when learning the "Secret of the Seers" is to get the subject into what is called a Habituated Compliance mind set with what is known as Yes Set. A Yes Set is a Numinations fundamental and a type of repetition cycle where the sole intention is to cause Disassociated Control so the listener will repeat the word yes or give some kind of confirmation multiple times to a few cleverly created statements of obvious truths. The purpose in creating this Conditioned Agreement mind set is to get the person you are talking to into an unconscious pattern of affirming whatever is said through the act of repeatedly saying yes (or another Confirmation) when you are speaking to them. The conditioned mind then becomes a controlled mind, because it conforms to the sequence. The mind repeats the thoughts and phrases then begins to think in the pattern. In the end what you are doing is conditioning the listeners mind to agree to your assertions.

While applying the (Conditioning Agreement) Yes Set you may want to accentuate your statements by adding a little up and down nod of the head, like a shaking

172

your head in a yes, while making your assertions to the subject. This will add a tremendous amount of power to the conditioning of the subject to the desired state of mind. When implanting your Yes Set on your subject it is also recommended that you use guiding questions.

Guiding questions are when you string a few lines of questions together that can be associated to what you want the listener to eventually say yes to. You see a listener may not normally want to say yes to what ever you are going to ask if you said it first but if you string it along with some other questions that are related the subject will be more inclined to do so.

Example:

1. You said you like to ski, right?
2. So, you like breathing in the clean air in the mountains?
3. I bet it's sometimes a bit harder on you lungs at those altitudes?
4. So it is probably safe to say smoking while you Ski could make it a bit harder?

Now when you want your Yes Sets to be even more effective you will want to use what I like to call obvious truths and make them in statements not questions. We will go over the reason for making it a statement in a moment but first let us examine obvious truths. An obvious truth is something that you know for certain is true or know the subject will at least perceive as true. Obvious truths make the subject easier to guide by creating Habituated Compliance within the listeners mind. Here are some examples of obvious truths to move one's intended subject into a conditioned Yes Set.

Note: I am going to use some universal statements below because there are others beside yourself who just might happen to be reading these words in another one of these books somewhere. So I want to use statements that address everyone in a more thorough way.

Example:
1. You can see these words?
2. Your heart is beating?
3. Sometimes you think to yourself?
4. And you can imagine all the different possibilities?

Those four preceding statements are all universal truths. One would be hard pressed to find a case where the previous statements are not true and therefore they will predictably command a positive reply of some kind from one's intended subject. Simultaneously it is conditioning compliance.

Section 2:

It's All in How You Ask

It is an understanding that when using the Jedi Mind Trick the Jedi adopt a peculiar tone of voice along with specific body language to emphasize certain key words (like nodding of the head in a yes motion). At this time the listener that is now a recipient to the Mind Trick and usually will go into a light trance and adopt a relaxed tone of voice with a dilated gaze. Stay acute and use Force Listening because this particular tone of voice is an important element to notice when performing the Secret of the Seer, because you are going to mimic it. Later we will be going over some basics in how to apply it as well.

You may notice that in the earlier examples from the previous section that there were four statements (*re-posted below*). If you look even more closely at these examples you may also notice that there happens to be question marks at the end of all four of these same said statements. One might even ask oneself, "Why did they do that? That doesn't seem to make much sense." As we know The Force does not follow the laws of convention nor does it the rules of language. The language rules of The Force differ slightly from the structure of regular language and the question marks were put there purposefully.

1. You said you like to ski, right?

2. So, you like breathing in the clean air in the mountains?

3. I bet it's sometimes a bit harder on you lungs at those altitudes?

4. So it is probably safe to say smoking while you Ski could make it a bit harder?

The rationale behind putting the question marks behind the statements was that even though one is making a statement, one's tonality must project the statement as if they are merely asking a simple question, as for the Yes Set. This specific procedure utilizes preprogrammed social conditioning processes that are already contained in your subject's psyche. This makes receiving yes's from the listener much more effortless, while also binding your statement at the same time.

The psychological factors working behind the method being used is that the statements in the examples are unconsciously posed as both question and statement in the mind of the subject and therefore binding the statement and creating a Feint. This subsequently causes a subtle confusion within the listener's subconscious mind. This confusion works to one's advantage by creating two avenues upon which thought can be directed. If the statement is incorrect, one was merely asking a simple question. Conversely if the statement is accurate it will trigger the listener's conformation bias and

176

one will appear to be incredibly profound to the listener or anyone nearby close enough to take notice. This can be quite useful when spreading your sphere of influence to others and helping The Force grow.

Here is another Force Power one should employ that will add another dimension to one's skill. This other dimension will also add a greater amount of validity to the statement one has posed to their intended subject. It is not necessary yet it is preferred that you make use of the Numonic skill of a Noncommittal Feint within the statement that you wish to impress upon someone. A Noncommittal Feint is a phrase that predicts a demographic probability about the subject without committing to what was actually said. This is preferred because of its ability to produce an outwardly assumed precise statement while at the same time leaving open the possibility to change the subject matter to a comparatively different topic.

Example:

1. You probably like Science fiction?

2. You tend to be somewhat of a dreamer?

The previously mentioned statements however are not truly committed statements and are in all actuality only a few educated guesses or Feints. These subtly Noncommittal Feints, when correct, will establish the impression of one having a mysterious foresight and unworldly abilities. If the statement is incorrect it is irrelevant because what you said was never committed to in the statement in the first place. It's as if you have made a hidden back door to your own statement.

Let us review:

1. You want to get your Subject into a Yes Set or some type of Condition Agreement.

2. You will do this by stating obvious facts and/or Feints (educated guesses posed as questions but are actually statements.)

3. You are going to repeat this procedure several times.

4. You can use Noncommittal phrases for an easy out if your assertion is not confirmed.

Remember to use the previously mentioned techniques consistently especially when you choose to pose a question and/or statement and still wants to be perceived as mysterious and exceptionally insightful.

Section 3:

If They Don't Confirm Your Statement

From time to time when making a statement one may not get the confirmation that one is looking for from their intended subject. One may actually run into a few obstacles and get someone who is a bit uncertain about the assertions you posed. One may even get a certain person who totally negates the statement altogether. For some would-be Force Masters this could be a troublesome burden, nevertheless when one is learning the ways of The Force, minor inconveniences such as someone not complying with a statement can be simply brushed off with ease. Let me show you how.

First I would like to address the type of subject who will either be suspicious of or confused by your statement(s). Subjects that do either of these things or only partially agree with the statement will usually give verbal clues to their misunderstanding. This is a time to condition your Force Listening skills because believe it or not, these clues that the listener will give you are the very same kinds of words that were covered in the previous section. These clues that the listener will be using are the same Noncomittal words and/or phrases you just used yourself and that are explained in the Numinations section of this book.

The reason for this happens is that the subject is unsure and cannot commit to your statement about them because they themselves are skeptical or are just plain uncertain. To help guide you along the path when you hear a Noncommittal you should always address the subject's Noncommittal word or phrase with a strategic combination of other words from the Numonic Lexicon they are the Confirmation and the Link.

A Link is a word that links two thoughts together in some form or fashion. Words like; and, plus, also and moreover are Links. You get the picture. The Link is an excellent way to direct your subject to another assertion. Look at the examples:

1. You: You tend (Noncommittal) to be timid at times?

Subject: Maybe… (Noncommittal)

You: (Interrupt) of course (Conformation), and (Link) sometimes that timid demeanor goes away in the face of adversity?

2. You: You probably (Noncommittal) like to draw?

Subject: Well sometimes (Noncommittal) I do.

You: Sure (Conformation) and (Link) that core creative mindset will also lead you to create many magnificent things in life.

This is relatively easy for one to master. All one has to remember is that when the subject says any Noncommittal word or phrase the retort will always be a Confirmation followed by a Link to the next statement.

Let us review:

1. You will use Force Listening to hear a Noncommittal coming from the Subject.

2. You will address the Noncomittal with a Confirmation and Link.

3. You are then going to change subject matters to a different yet associated subject matter.

Now we are going to address an extremely important problem that can occur fairly often with different people. That is a Negation. This is when a person blatantly says No, Wrong, You don't know, or some other out right rejection. These Negations tend to sometimes test one's metal however they are something one will be commonly be running into while using Force Influence powers. Over time one will become accustomed to dealing with these rebuttals as one becomes more familiar with using these and other Force Sensory skills and handling these rebuts will be like child's play to you.

One of the best things to remember while learning these skills is to just recognize the subject's negations as only a contest to what one is saying. Contests can sometimes be a bit of a challenge however winning competitions definitely has some great rewards. Challenges make ones core stronger and this will help you become even influential at commanding The Force. So make it fun and rise up to the challenge of the competition it will help you stay calm in the face of adversity. Conviction in your statements is key to rising above the challenge.

The first thing you have to remember is really pretty easy it is to merely change the subjects Negation into a Noncomittal. The best way in which one will approach this task is by using specific group of Numonic words which are called Bridges. Bridges are words and phrases like But, However, Though and Nevertheless, to name a few. These words and phrases should be the first thing said after one has heard any kind of Negation uttered by the subject. The reason for this is that it gives you an opportunity to backtrack and redefine what was implied by you're first statement.

Next you will want to make a similar claim to your original statement or a claim with a subject that relates in some way shape or form to the original statement (note: You will want to employ the same rules used previously to produce the first statement). Within the new statement one will also add a Numonic word form the group of words called Realizers to help more smoothly guide the subject's mindset to a Noncomittal reaction. A Realizer is a Phrase or sentence that brings a thought into realization within the subject. Words such as Realize, Aware, Recognize, Notice, and, Identify.

Example:

1.You: I have an intuition about you.

Subject: What's that?

You: You seem (Noncommittal) to have a tendency to want to be better than you really are?

Subject: No (Negation) not (Negation) really I am quite content with what I am doing.

You: Although (Bridge) you may be saying this now, you may not realize (Realizer) that a set of circumstances are coming in the near future that will actually change this point of view.

Subject: Maybe (Noncommittal)…

Now this will give you the ability to go back and change the now Noncommittal back into a Confirmation, like you just learned earlier in this section.

Let us review:

1. The subject Negates your Feint.

2. You then use and Bridge paired with a Realizer.

3. You will repeat the above two steps in different forms until you hear a Noncommittal from the subject.

4. You will then proceed as if it were a Noncommittal.

Believe it or not it is that simple.

Section 4:

The Force Binds Us

As we know The Force is a tie that binds all living things and it is important to know that because of this we have similar challenges that face us in life. Many people have to deal with numerous challenges throughout their life and many of those challenges involve issues dealing with Health, Economics, or Relationships. These are universal hardships that most of us must experience to understand the real meaning of The Force and because of this you can use these issues as a marker for your feints when using Force intuition.

Let me explain how, lets say you use a Yes Set (Conditioning Agreement) and then make a feint to impress upon someone your Force Intuition skills. As explained earlier your feint may not be on target or well received so you in turn use the tools that you have learned from the Secret of the Seers so far and use them to redirect the subjects focus. When you first start the easiest way to change the focus that you will direct the listener to is to use one of the binding challenges that we all share (It is quite effective to use them as your original feint as well.) being Health, Economics, or Relationships. This is because those three binding challenges can also be connected to each other to some degree or another.

Example 1:

You: "You have been having some stomach issues, haven't you?"

Subject: "<u>Not</u> (Negation) that I know of."

You: "Perhaps you may not be <u>aware</u> (Realizer) of it now <u>however</u> (Bridge) there is something in your life that is causing you stress that could lead up to these stomach issues in the future. Perhaps it is a problem with a friend or someone from work that has been eating away at you?"

Subject: "Well <u>maybe </u>(Noncommittal)."

You: "<u>That's right</u> (Conformation) <u>and </u>(Link)…"

If you notice the first feint is about Health and it is not a hit so I use the Secret of the Seers to maneuver it to another universal challenge, being Relationships. Here is another example.

Example 2:

You: "I have an intuition that you <u>might</u> (Noncommittal) be having some financial difficulty at the moment."

Subject: "<u>No</u> (Negation) what do you mean I just won the lottery!"

You: "You may have just won the lottery <u>nevertheless</u> (Equalizer) you must <u>recognize</u> (Realizer) that many of your friends and acquaintances are going to be affected by this."

Subject: "I <u>could</u> (Noncommittal) see that."

You: "<u>Yes</u> (Conformation) you can, <u>and</u> (Link)…"

Again these universal issues are the ties that bind us together. One must take into consideration that we are not all as different as we think and appreciate the fact that we are more the less same. This is a basic understanding of The Force and why this aspect to the technique is so powerful, because The Force is part of all living things, it is the ebb and it is the flow, it is the night and the day. Recognize The Force is within you and then your ability to understand and channel its power will become second nature to you

186

Section 5:

Equations to the Secret of the Seers

In this section we are going to break down the Secret of the Seer for you into a three step process and then show you it in a diagram form for you to better understand how it works and its application.

First: Use a series of (Conditioning Agreement) Yes sets up to a Noncomittal Feint (If subject is unsure go to the next step, if subject Negates go to Third step, if accepted keep going on with the subject matter use subjective validation to you benefit.)

Second: Use a Conformation and a Link as rebut to the Noncomittal and switch to an associated subject matter from there. Again you should use subjective validation to your benefit in these matters

Third: Use a Bridge then a Realizer to switch the subject matter as to get listener to say a Noncomittal and then go to the third step.

This is the basic structure behind of the Secret of the Seer. Although the words of the technique are simple, and the actions easily performed, it is not in the words that you speak that give it its power. It is your intent behind them that creates that mystical connection between you and The Force. If your mind is corrupt then your results will in turn be corrupt. By chasing external rewards, one will lose power over life, and end up becoming a reactionary instrument of circumstance.

"Remember: Your focus determines your reality"

Qui-Gon Jinn

Greatness comes through the way of The Force and following its guidance. Only then can you feel the intimate connection that is created by using The Force and the Secret of the Seer.

Chapter 6:

Final Understandings of The Force and its Powers

It has been repeated numerous times throughout this book that with an understanding of how The Force works there comes a great amount of self discipline that needs to be applied. It is repeated because of its importance to the discipline. The awareness of the oneness of all things must always be taken into consideration when applying The Force. Ignite the field of acceptance around everything in your awareness and the way of The Force will come to you more naturally.

One must practice being aware because it will reveal to you that which keeps one form their natural connection to The Force and all things. It is not without trepidations or hardships for many but put aside imprudent reservations or unforeseen fears for The

189

Force is strong and will guide you to a new revelation into who you really are and what you really are able to accomplish. Our conditioned illusions of identity, assumptions and responses are what keep us from being one with The Force and they imprison us in a fantasy of our own vanity. They separate us from the wholeness of what is The Force.

So one must ask oneself, "How does one tell the difference between what the conditioned mind is telling me and what the connected mind is explaining." Ones answer will always be "Only through the practice of The Force will this challenge become clearer." and practice you must. In this last chapter we will touch on the beliefs behind the power of The Force. We will examine what it really is to readjust our minds so we can use The Force more efficiently and flow with it so we can be a part of its masterful field of energy.

Section 1:

The Use of Non-Force Equals Access to The Force:

Our knowledge and experiences are real to us however reality has many forms. This may cause some complications at times for the mind is limited by the memory of oneself and the sensory input connected with it. By applying the skills in this book appropriately one can expand oneself beyond the barriers of such challenges and in doing so experience the power that truly is The Force.

190

Certain manifestations of The Force can be learned through knowledge and words whereas further manifestations come from intellectual, creative and reflexive thinking, nevertheless if one could move in the exact opposite direction and completely leave such intellectual intent altogether one would be able to actually experience the full beauty of The Force in and of it self. This seems counter intuitive but alas it is the way of The Force and it is how The Force is channeled.

All the living forms are naturally connected and filled with The Force however many of us become reactionary and lose track of its guiding power. That is why we must train in the discipline of The Force.

 Remember when you were you were younger and something inside of you told you that you shouldn't do this or that but you did it anyway, later to find out that little something inside of you was right. That moment was a little glimmer of when you were connected to The Force and The Force was speaking directly to you. This is the reason why intellectual intent can keep us form the amazing power of The Force. We tend to rationalize things and try not to believe the unbelievable. Imagine going back in time and telling someone form the Dark Ages that you have flown thousands of feet up in the air in what is called an airplane. You would probably be burned alive at the stake for being a witch or some other supernatural being. This is because the minds of those people could not fathom the ability to do those kinds of things.

Just like the people from ages ago many people today will not be able to fathom the teachings in this book as well. Some people after reading this book will even deny that these techniques work on them even though throughout this book there have been numerous neurological studies to the contrary. This is because many do not want to believe that they are not in full control of their mind. Many do not want to believe that outside influences have an affect on it everyday in numerous ways. They want to feel as if they have control, that they make their own choices all the time and that their mind is never on automatic pilot. As you see Selective Validation rears its ugly head again, it is natural and there is nothing wrong with it, but learn to understand it and use it as a tool to help you grow. Step away from getting caught up with the trivial aspects of ones existence then your mind will revert back to equanimity and thus become more in touch with the higher consciousness that resides inside you. This alone will bring you to a level where others will think of you as a supernatural being even now in today's world.

Section 2:

Conditioning and The Force

In this book conditioning is a major contributor in the implementation of The Force. The use of others conditioning is a key element to many of The Force techniques.

As we have seen throughout this book the Conditioned mind can fall prey to countless suggestions and associations that can affect the experience of ones reality. That is why reconditioning of one own mind is imperative to be able to become more in touch with The Force. Reconditioning ones own mind helps one understand reality as it is, not as what others have trained or socialized you to believe. Remember mass conditioning is the enemy of The Force. Here is a question you may have heard before "If everyone jumped off a cliff would you do it?" The answer one would think would be an emphatic "No!" however with the conditioned mind that is not always the case. So take a step back and think about what kind of conditioned responses of "jumping off a cliff" that may be the standard way of thinking in this modern era and maybe even some you may fall prey to. Are certain cars actually, in the literal sense, sexy and if so what is it about an automobile that would induce a biological feeling of wanting to reproduce, seems like that might be just a little bit absurd thought when you really think about it. For many of us that idea has been conditioned into our minds since we were children and so we accept it. Remember it was accepted knowledge for most of human history that the sun revolved around the earth and we all know very well that that was not true. One must learn how to look within ones self sometimes instead of outside one self and realize if they themselves created a belief or was it impressed upon them by an external source. So just take a step back and be mindful of whether you have chosen to think something for yourself or whether it was conditioned. The answers might surprise you.

That being said some people may think that the use of this book and its tactics may be considered manipulative by evaluating only the surface structure instead of the deeper intention of it. That is only the superficial socially conditioned mind speaking not the open and transcending mind. The superficial mind has an inability to see what the open mind can see and that is while using The Force you open other people up to the awareness of its power and a deeper understanding of interpersonal connections. You also are reconditioning yourself to be conscious of the subconscious communications going on between yourself and others. While you are becoming more enlightened to subconscious communication you are also given the ability to recognize when it is being used on you. This in turn allows you to transcend your current level of awareness and conditioning to bring you to a higher realm of consciousness, which is the core element behind the power of The Force.

Many try so hard yet in vain to live their lives without understanding what it is too truly see. Higher consciousness helps us see how The Force itself is mirrored in our own individual structure, and invites us to live in a direct relationship with it. What the issue is, is nothing less than the activation of The Force within us, a movement towards higher consciousness. This consciousness is meant to break the afflictions caused by social conditioning and touch others in ways beyond the conditioned minds understanding.
This way may seem strikingly opposed to many of the misguided concepts of the externally conditioned minds beliefs yet virtue is an action that comes from within not from without. The way to The Force stems form this greater more deeply rooted internal form of morality, the morality of higher consciousness, a quality of awareness that is

based in a virtue that transcends our basic understandings.

To put it simply the principal intention of a Force practitioner is to seek a higher level of consciousness and pass onto others what they understand of that which is The Force through use of its techniques. By looking within oneself one can better come to understand that which is the power of The Force.

Section 3:

The Duality of The Force

The conditioned reality we live in is one of opposites. Every coin comes with two sides there is no good with out bad, there is no up with out down, there is not love without hate. The Force's understandings are beyond our rudimentary ideas of these concepts. Even though it may be practical to recognize that everything that one sees has its direct opposite, our challenge is to recognize that both sides of the coin are still just the coin. By clinging to one side more than another we in turn reject the other and thus are not acting with The Force. Acceptance is fundamental to The Force and acceptance of The Force transcends the conditioned concept of duality and accepts that they are both necessary elements of that which exists within us all.

There are some people whose conditioned minds may think that these understandings can be used to justify their self indulgences and rationalizations for callousness to others, however this is a misunderstanding of what truly is the power of The Force and is quite a dangerous way of interpreting things. The wise understand the harmonization of the two seemingly opposite sides. Only the foolish identify with one side or the other and do not reach beyond the limits of our understanding. A small mind tends to operate within the rules of duality; it sees things in only black and white, knowing boundaries, needing to be understood, resisting change, judging others, fearing death and in so doing life. These thoughts create friction and in so doing conflict. This is not the flowing vitality which is The Force and the wise recognize this.

With The Force there is no confusion between should I or should I not, to have or to have not. It is the actual process of the how, that is what The Force teaches us, because the act of evaluating is far different than the process of actualization. The actualization is what enables one to be able to make use of The Force. One cannot understand the full meaning or true qualities of The Force itself by quantifying the differences of how it is manifested to us. Only by acceptance of The Force can one truly understand The Force.

That being said it is wise to be steadfast in all that you do. Do not over analyze that which "is" for confusion will be your own undoing. Judge not the reality in which you live and learn to believe the unbelievable, accept the unacceptable, realize the unreal, and know the unknown. This is how you will become more powerful than you have ever known, but realize this with great power comes great responsibility. There are only a few who can get to the point where they can open up this new understanding and truly know the immense power one is capable of. You have the understandings and you have completed this book but this is just the beginning of your journey. So act with wisdom, cleanse yourself of social convention, and be steadfast in all that you do.

And remember "May The Force be with you…Always!"

Bibliography:

Raz Amir – Selective Biasing of a Specific Bistable-figure Percept Involves fMRI Signal Changes in Frontostriatal Circuits (American Journal of Clinical Hypnosis October, 2007)

John A Bargh, Marc Chen and Lara Burrows – Automaticity of Social Behavior: Direct Effects of Trait Construct and Stereo Type Activation on Action. (Journal of Personality and Social Psychology vol. 71 #2 1996)

John A. Bargh, Ran R. Hassin and James S. Ulemanand– The New Unconscious: Social Cognition and Social Neuroscience (Oxford University Press, 2006)

David Bohm – On Dialog (Routledge, 1996)

David Bohm – Thought as a System (Routledge, 1994)

James Braid – Braid on Hypnotism: The Beginnings of Modern Hypnosis (Julian Press, 1960)

Terry Brooks – Star Wars I: The Phantom Menace (Random House Publishing Group. 2000)

Robert T. Carroll – The Skeptic's Dictionary: A Collection of Strange Beliefs, Amusing Deceptions, and Dangerous Delusions (Wiley, 2003)

Robert B. Cialdini – Influence: The Psychology of Persuasion (Collins Business Essentials December 26, 2006)

Noam Chomsky – On Language (New Press, 1998)

Noam Chomsky – Language and Mind (Houghton Mifflin Harcourt P, 1972)

Tony Corinda – 13 Steps to Mentalism (Robbins Publication, 1996)

Paul Ekman – Unmasking the Face (Malor Books, 2003)

Paul Ekman and Friesen – Facial Action Coding System, (Consulting Psychologists Press, Inc., 1978)

Milton H. Erickson, Sheila I. Rossi, and Ernest L. Rossi – Hypnotic Realities: The Induction of Clinical Hypnosis and Forms of Indirect Suggestion. (Halsted Press, 1976) George H. Estabrooks – Hypnotism (Plume, 1959)

Jonathan Evans – Bias in Human Reasoning: Causes and Consequences (Psychology Press, 1990)

Bertram R Forer – The Fallacy of Personal Validation: A Classroom Demonstration of Gullibility (Journal of Abnormal and Social Psychology 44, 1949)

Gerd Gigerenzer – Simple Heuristics that Make Us Smart (Oxford University Press, 2000)

Malcolm Gladwell – Blink: The Power of Thinking without Thinking (Back Bay Books, 2007)

Donald F Glut, George Lucas – Star Wars V: The Empire Strikes Back (Random House Publishing Group. 1985)

David Gordon – Phoenix: Therapeutic Patterns of Milton H. Erickson (Meta Publications, 1981)

John Grinder and Richard Bandler – Trance-formations: Neuro-Linguistic Programming and the Structure of Hypnosis (Real People Press, 1981)

John Grinder and Richard Bandler – Patterns 1: Of the Hypnotic Techniques of Milton H. Erickson (Meta Publications, 1975)

John Grinder, Judith DeLozier and Richard Bandler – Patterns 2: Of the Hypnotic Techniques of Milton H. Erickson (Meta Publications, 1977)

Eckhard Hess – The Tell Tail Eye: How Your Eyes Reveal Hidden Thoughts and Emotions (Van Nostrand Reinhold Co.1975)

James Kahn – Star Wars VI: Return of the Jedi (Random House Publishing Group. 1983)

Thomas E. Kida – Don't Believe Everything You Think: The 6 Basic Mistakes We Make in Thinking (Prometheus Books, 2006)

Alfred Korzybski – Science and Sanity: An Introduction to Non-Aristotelian Systems and General Semantics (Institute of General Semantics, 1995)

Robert V. Levine – The Power of Persuasion: How we're Bought and Sold (Wiley, 2003)

George Lucas – Star Wars IV: A New Hope (Random House Publishing Group. 1986)

David Marks and Richard Kammann- The Psychology of the Psychic (Prometheus Books, 1979)

Phil Merikle and Meredyth Daneman – Psychological Investigations of Unconscious Perception (Journal of Consciousness Studies #5 1998)

Desmond Morris – Manwatching: A Field Guide to Human Behavior (Harry N Abrams, 1979)

Desmond Morris – The Naked Ape: A Zoologist's Study of the Human Animal (Delta, 1999)

Robert A. Nelson – The Art of Cold Reading (Hades Publication Inc, 1989)

Steven Pinker – The Stuff of Thought: Language as a Window into Human Nature (Viking, 2007)

Richard Restak – Mozart's Brain and the Fighter Pilot (Three Rivers Press, 2002)

Giacomo Rizzolatti, Corrado Sinigaglia and Frances Anderson – Mirrors in the Brain: How Our Minds Share Actions, Emotions, and Experience (Oxford University Press, 2008)

Giacomo Rizzolatti, Stanislas Dehaene, Jean-René Duhamel and Marc D. Hauser – From Monkey Brain to Human Brain: A Fyssen Foundation Symposium (The MIT Press, 2005)

Giacomo Rizzolatti, Pier Francesco Ferrari, Vittorio Gallese, and Leonardo Fogassi – Mirror Neurons Responding to the Observation of Ingestive and Communicative Mouth Actions in the Monkey Ventral Premotor Cortex. (European Journal of Neuroscience, 17 (8), 2003)

Anthony Robbins – Unlimited Power: The New Science of Personal Achievement (Free Press, 1997)

Sydney Rosen – My Voice Will Go With You: The Teaching Tales of Milton H. Erickson (W. W. Norton & Company, 1991)

Tali Sharot, Mauricio R Delgado & Elizabeth A Phelps – How emotion enhances the feeling of remembering (Nature Neuroscience 7, 1376 - 1380 2004)

R. A. Salvatore – Star Wars II: Attack of the Clones (Random House Publishing Group. 2003)

Carol Somer – Conversational Hypnosis: A Manual of Indirect Suggestion (Paperback) Sommer Solutions, Inc. (October 1992)

Matthew Stover – Star Wars III: Revenge of the Sith (Random House Publishing Group. 2005)

Richard Webster – Quick and Effective Cold Reading (Brookfield Press, 1988)

Leonard Zusne and Warren H. Jones – Anomalistic Psychology: A Study of Magical Thinking (Lawrence Erlbaum, 1989)

ISBN-13: 978-1519480248
ISBN-10: 1519480245